100

THINGS TO DO IN
ALBUQUERQUE
BEFORE YOU
DIE

100
THINGS TO DO IN
ALBUQUERQUE
BEFORE YOU
DIE

ASHLEY M. BIGGERS

Library of Congress Control Number: 2015930936

ISBN: 9781681060064

Design by Jill Halpin

Printed in the United States of America
15 16 17 18 19   5 4 3 2 1

Please note that websites, phone numbers, addresses, and company names are subject to change or cancellation. We did our best to relay the most accurate information available, but due to circumstances beyond our control, please do not hold us liable for misinformation. When exploring new destinations, please do your homework before you go.

CONTENTS

• •

• •

PREFACE

I'm one of the rare Albuquerqueans who was born, raised, and lives in my hometown. I love that the Duke City—whether through the film industry, Sandia National Laboratories, Kirtland Air Force Base, University of New Mexico, or myriad other reasons—beckons people from across the United States and the world. In some cases, those transplants explore more of the city than locals. I've met many Albuquerqueans who comment that there's nothing to do here. I, for one, never have enough time for all the places I want to go and events I want to attend.

So when I began writing *100 Things to Do in Albuquerque Before You Die*, I wanted to capture all the enthralling aspects of the city I love, from the obvious picks to the offbeat ones. Yes, you'll find the Sandia Peak Tramway, Old Town, and the Isotopes here—but I hope you'll also discover the unexpected, quirky, and cultural places and happenings that make Albuquerque such a dynamic place.

This list isn't meant to be rankings from first to worst. Instead, it's meant to be a collection of 100 things that will give you insight into the Duke City—and to inspire you to keep exploring. Beyond the full list, you'll also find seasonal itineraries and those for several interest areas, including for foodies, families, and outdoor enthusiasts. Because Albuquerque sits in the heart of New Mexico, I've also included a few road trips that will take you beyond the city limits to explore this matchless region.

If there are ABQ musts I haven't mentioned here, let me know on Facebook at facebook.com/100ThingsABQ. I want to hear from you!

I hope your adventures are *all* good! Bueno, bye.

—Ashley M. Biggers

ACKNOWLEDGMENTS

To my parents, Kelley McCausland, and Bob and Cyndee Biggers, who taught me that, in my hometown, there's always something new to discover.

FOOD
AND DRINK

CHOW DOWN
ON A GREEN-CHILE CHEESEBURGER

Barbecue is to Texas as green-chile cheeseburgers are to New Mexico. This down-home classic is synonymous with the state. Every local has his or her favorite spot for a burger, and there are many competition-worthy plates. Each September there's a burger battle royale at the New Mexico State Fair, and the State of New Mexico Department of Tourism even created a Green-Chile Cheeseburger Trail so those with a hankering for gooey chile and cheese can get their fix in every corner of the Land of Enchantment. Holy Cow Burgers serve Albuquerque's best version in a modern diner ambiance. The burger's hearty patty uses New Mexico–grown beef. It's grilled to juicy, smoky perfection, then piled high with not-too-hot, roasted green chile and real cheddar cheese on a toasted bun that holds up under all that, well, burger. Top it with perfectly crispy bacon for a tough-to-beat dish. Add hand-cut fries on the side (just like mama makes) and a chocolate shake for the full mouth-watering meal.

700 Central Ave., SE, 505-242-2991, holycownm.com

Neighborhood: EDo
Kid Friendly

TIP

Grab the best vegetarian variety
in the city at Flying Star Café, then
go-to meet-up spot for locals that boasts
a to-die-for dessert case.
The MOO-ve Over Meat Veggie Burger
features a spicy black-bean patty, cheddar
cheese, and Cajun dressing on a Challah bun.
Ask to top it with chopped green chile for
a satisfying burger that vegetarians, and
perhaps even carnivores, will adore.
Nine locations, flyingstarcafe.com

DINE FINE
AT JENNIFER JAMES 101

Jennifer James is in a class of her own as Albuquerque's celebrity chef. For five consecutive years (2010–2015), the James Beard Foundation named her a semifinalist for its Best Chef: Southwest Award, no other Albuquerque chef has been so honored. The awards are considered the culinary equivalent of the Oscars, and this self-taught chef certainly serves star-worthy dishes. Of course, the seasonal menu is always changing, but past editions have included Korean-style pork belly with radish kimchi and ginger-scallion sauce, and crispy-skin duck with soft polenta and pomegranate. The restaurant's name reflects James's desire for back-to-basics cooking that allows her local, seasonal ingredients to truly sing.

4615 Menaul Blvd., NE, 505-884-3860, jenniferjames101.com

Neighborhood: Uptown

TIP
Although the fine-dining meals here are worth every penny, the restaurant also serves three-course, $25 Thursday dinners. Check the website for the menu and be sure to make advance reservations.

DRIZZLE HONEY
ON A SOPAIPILLA

Honey dripping down your fingers and arms is a sign you're enjoying these puffs of dough fried to crispy perfection. Casa de Benavidez, a family restaurant that's been serving in the Duke City for more than fifty years, has some of the best in the city. There isn't a bad dish on the menu here, but the sopaipillas are tops. The restaurant, which offers serene patio dining beneath cottonwood trees during the summer, also serves savory versions stuffed with fajita meat, carne adovada, beef, beans, or chicharrónes (fried pork rinds).

8032 Fourth St., NW, 505-898-3311, casadebenavidez.com

Neighborhood: North Valley
Kid friendly

TIP

Although it's not officially on the morning menu, ask your server for a stuffed sopaipilla. The breakfast version is stuffed with scrambled eggs, hash browns, and cheese, and is topped with red or green chile and more cheddar.

Another Sopaipilla to Savor: Sadie's of New Mexico, four locations, sadiesofnewmexico.com

SIP A MARGARITA
FROM ZACATECAS

The margarita is a signature of the Southwest—just as the mint julep is in the Southeast. Zacatecas serves the best in Albuquerque. The house ZACArita is a perfect blend of sweet and sour. If you want a bit more sizzle, try the Chalchihuitl, which is mixed with poblano-infused tequila. Even if the dozen or so menu options don't appeal, you can build your own by choosing your favorite tequila and liqueur, which the bartender will then shake with agave nectar and fresh lime juice. If you need something to wash down your cocktail, this taco joint was a James Beard Award semi-finalist for Best New Restaurant in 2013.

3423 Central Ave., NE, 505-255-8226, zacatecastacos.com

Neighborhood: Nob Hill

TEAR OFF A PIECE
OF A FRONTIER SWEET ROLL

Frontier Restaurant has been an Albuquerque institution since it opened in 1971—perhaps because it has served so many locals during their stints at the University of New Mexico, which is just across Central Avenue. But post-graduate diners eat here, too, and locals have named it best for "late-night eats" and "cheap eats" in alt-weekly reader polls. The barn-like restaurant is open from 5 a.m. to 1 a.m., seven days a week, which means diners can order signature dishes such as green-chile stew, homemade flour tortillas, and carne adovada nearly any time. The apex of the Frontier menu, however, is the Sweet Roll, which was featured on the Travel Channel's *Man v. Food.* The pastry's fluffy folds are coated with sugar and drenched with butter, making them as crave-worthy as anything you'll ever eat. So, grab a table near a portrait of John Wayne (the owners have an affinity for portraits of The Duke) and pull off an edge of the sweet roll's spiral. The rolls are also available at the four locations of Golden Pride, which Frontier Restaurant owners Larry and Dorothy Rainosek also operate.

2400 Central Ave., SE, 505-266-0550, frontierrestaurant.com

Neighborhood: University
Kid Friendly

BREAKFAST
AT BARELAS COFFEE HOUSE

Rachael Ray dined at this eatery for her Food Network Show *$40 a Day*, giving a nod to the restaurant's affordable menu. However, you're more likely to find neighborhood residents dining here than celebrity chefs. Brothers James and Michael Gonzales opened the eatery in 1978, and their sister Benita Villaneuva joined them quickly thereafter. Their family has lived in the Barelas neighborhood, one of the city's oldest neighborhoods, for four generations, and the restaurant is a testament to the family's longtime connections there. Here, servers know the names of every vecino (elderly person) and regular who enters the casual diner's doors. Movers and shakers meet here for out-of-the-office deal making. Local publications' readers' polls regularly acknowledge the cuisine here as city favorites, including huevos rancheros deliciously smothered in chile and authentic dishes such as menudo (a traditional soup made with beef tripe).

1502 Fourth St., SW, 505-843-7577, on Facebook

Neighborhood: Barelas
Kid Friendly

PICK RASPBERRIES
AT HEIDI'S RASPBERRY FARM

Heidi's Raspberry Jam—or, even better Raspberry Red-Chile Jam—is a staple in Albuquerqueans' pantries. Come fall, so are the pints of farm-fresh berries, which are available at several local growers markets. However, there's little better than tasting the tart, luscious fruit straight from the hedges. The farm welcomes visitors to its five-acre u-pick fields in Los Lunas from mid-August through October (depending on the harvest and subsequent frost). The Corrales fields were replanted in 2014, and owner Heidi Eleftheriou hopes to open the four acres of raspberries and blackberries for u-pick in the future. The 10,000–20,000 pounds of berries per year Eleftheriou's fields produce are all organic.

600 Lindero del Drenaje, Corrales; 1 Sun Valley Rd., Los Lunas
505-898-1784, heidisraspberryjam.com

Neighborhood: Corrales and Los Lunas
Kid Friendly

TASTE THE FRUITS
OF LOCAL VINES

Although wine is now produced in all fifty states, few can claim this accolade: New Mexico is the oldest wine-producing region in the country—even before California. Franciscan monks planted the first grapevines here in 1629, near Socorro, just south of Albuquerque. European mission grapes are still grown in the state today, though most Duke City–area vintners stick to varietals more pleasing to the contemporary palate. Nine wineries and tasting rooms have cropped up in Albuquerque since the 1970s. Most notable among this group is Gruet Winery, whose founder, Laurent Gruet, relocated in 1984 from France and soon began producing wines according to the Méthode Champenoise. Gruet's sparkling wines have become the drink of choice for toasts throughout the city, but the praise extends beyond city limits. In 2011, the winery won silver at the San Diego International Wine Competition for the Gruet Extra Dry Blanc de Blancs.

8400 Pan American Freeway, NE, (888) 857-9463
505-857-0066, gruetwinery.com

Neighborhood: Northeast Heights

TIP

Casa Rondena Winery has the most scenic tasting room in the city. Nestled in the lush valley of Los Ranchos de Albuquerque, the stone building and sips of the winery's Meritage will transport you to Tuscany.

733 Chavez Rd., NW
505-344-5911
casarondena.com

NIBBLE A BISCOCHITO
AT GOLDEN CROWN PANADERIA

New Mexico's official state cookie, the biscochito, is an anise-flavored, cinnamon-sugar number traditionally served over Christmas. Golden Crown Panaderia makes some two thousand five hundred dozen each holiday season, but the Old Town neighborhood bakery makes them by hand year-round. Pratt Morales opened the bakery in 1972, today, he runs it with his son, Chris, who grew up baking alongside his father. When you walk into the adobe building bedecked with murals of hollyhocks, a server will hand you a crumbly biscochito to eat while you're sifting through the array of treats on the menu. For a gluten-free option, choose the blue-corn version. Golden Crown also serves sweet and savory empanadas, spicy chile bread, and made-to-order pizzas.

1103 Mountain Rd., NW, 505-243-2424, goldencrown.biz

Neighborhood: Old Town
Kid Friendly

BRUNCH
AT ELI'S PLACE

Formerly Sophia's Place, Eli's Place is a hole-in-the-wall joint whose dishes pack in big flavors—and big crowds. Triple D (*Diners, Drive-Ins and Dives* on the Food Network) fans will remember this North Valley destination as the home of eclectic dishes such as scallop tacos and spicy-duck enchiladas topped with tomatillo sauce. No matter the time of day you're eating here, it's hard to find a poor item on the menu. For weekend brunch, opt for the moist blue-corn pancakes topped with fresh fruit and piñon butter, with a side of crispy potatoes. The to-die-for breakfast burritos are smothered with some of the best chile in the city.

6313 Fourth St., NW, 505-345-3935, on Facebook

Neighborhood: North Valley
Kid Friendly

TIP

Because Eli's has only ten indoor tables, be prepared to wait. Dining here during the summer, when outdoor patio tables are available, will decrease the amount of time you have to linger without seating.

TOAST THE CITY'S
ROOFTOP BARS

Apothecary Lounge, atop Hotel Parq Central, offers panoramic views of the Sandia Mountains to the east and downtown to the west. Sunset viewing from the vantage is colorful, and all the more enjoyable with a Prohibition-era cocktail in hand. Cocoon-like couches mean you'll be tempted to stay a while to enjoy your Sazerac, Moscow Mule, or a cocktail featuring the Apothecary's wide selection of bitters. The lounge's interior décor plays up the sophisticated boutique hotel's past as a clinic, with hospital bed wheels grounding low glass tables.

806 Central Ave., SE, 505-242-0040, hotelparqcentral.com

Neighborhood: EDo

OTHER ROOFTOP
BARS OF NOTE

Ibiza at Hotel Andaluz

This second-story bar offers secluded tables and lounge-worthy couches with views of downtown and the Sandia Mountains.
125 Second St., NW, 505-242-9090
hotelandaluz.com

Seasons Rotisserie & Grill

This Old Town cantina serves killer cocktails and live music.
2031 Mountain Rd., NW, 505-766-5100
seasonsabq.com

BITE
INTO BUFFET'S CANDIES

Albuquerqueans go—pardon the pun—nuts for the piñon candies at Buffet's. George Buffet started the candy company in 1956 and the family still operates the business today. The building, with a large candy cane leaning up against it, has become a landmark, beckoning sweet-toothed locals in the door for nut confections made with the small, buttery piñons native to New Mexico (including toffee, horny toads, rolls, pralines, and brittles).

7001 Lomas Blvd., NE, 505-265-7731, buffetscandies.com

Neighborhood: Uptown
Kid Friendly

TAKE FIELD-TO-FORK
TO THE NEXT LEVEL AT FARM & TABLE

Local food may be all the rage, but it's a rare restaurant where you can see the field where your food is grown from your table. Farmer-in-residence Ric Murphy, of Sol Harvest, oversees the nine acres of alfalfa and two-acre produce farm behind Farm & Table. These fresh-from-the-field crops inspire, and are featured in, many of the restaurant's dishes. When the ingredients don't come directly from the farm, restaurateur Cheri Montoya Austin works with dozens of local purveyors to supply the rest. Her goal is that one hundred percent of the makings will be locally sourced, at the time of this writing, that goal is close at hand. Of course, the seasonal menu is always evolving. In the past it has featured lamb stew, mushroom-and-kale empanadas, and green-chile cheeseburgers—most at relatively affordable prices. During summer, the farm's patio is a city favorite for weekend brunches.

8917 Fourth St., NW, 505-503-7124, farmandtablenm.com

Neighborhood: North Valley
Kid Friendly

TIP
Farm & Table is set in a quaint adobe, with limited seating. Be sure to make a reservation, particularly on weekend evenings and special occasions.

LIVE LIKE A LOCAVORE
AT LOS POBLANOS HISTORIC INN & ORGANIC FARM

The fine-dining experience at La Merienda is all the more special thanks to Los Poblanos' contemporary charm and deep history. That past dates to the 1930s, when Congressman Albert Simms and his wife, Ruth Hanna McCormick Simms, resided on the farm, also home to the original Creamland Dairies (now a household name in Albuquerque). The couple commissioned John Gaw Meem, one of the state's most important architects, to design a Cultural Center that, when built, cemented the property's historic status. Today, Los Poblanos continues to operate that center, as well as an inn for guests, and a lavender and organic farm. Until a few years ago, the dining room was open only to guests of the inn, today, they still receive priority seating. Reservations are required for non-guests. In the hands of Executive Chef Jonathan Perno, a devotee of the Slow Food Movement and farm-to-table philosophy, the restaurant has evolved into one of the city's most memorable dining establishments. Perno's menus draw from the farm, including bacon and pork from its pigs, and honey from its bees, as well as from other purveyors in the Río Grande Valley. The ever-evolving menu has featured smoked Los Poblanos pork belly with local greens, red-wine braised short ribs, and a green-chile, root-vegetable ragout with parsnip and garlic sauce and topped with fried carrots and leeks. If your meal sparks star-chef aspirations, Los Poblanos offers one cooking class a month on topics such as bread making, cooking with honey, and desserts.

4803 Rio Grande Blvd., NW, 505-344-9297, lospoblanos.com

Neighborhood: Los Ranchos de Albuquerque

TIP

To enjoy a cocktail in the Sala Grande living room, arrive fifteen to twenty minutes prior to your reservation time. La Merienda's handcrafted cocktails incorporate Spanish sherries, Italian vermouths, and—as should be expected here—farm-fresh ingredients.

EXPLORE THE FRONTIER
OF BEER

New Mexico is the Frontier of Beer, at least according to the New Mexico Brewers Guild's apt tag line. While off the map of many beer connoisseurs (this is rapidly changing), the brewers here have had the freedom to experiment and push their flavors to new heights. This is particularly true in Albuquerque, which has fifteen breweries or tap rooms in the city proper at the time of this writing (some have more than one location). In 2014, the New Mexico state legislature named a largely industrial neighborhood as Albuquerque's Brewery District. It includes Canteen Brewhouse (formerly Il Vicino Brewery), La Cumbre Brewing, and Nexus Brewery. One of the city's top breweries, Marble Brewery, lies outside of these boundaries. Albuquerque is an IPA town, so be sure to sample this variety.

For more info: nmbeer.org

NOTABLE BREWERIES

Canteen Brewhouse (formerly Il Vicino Brewery)
The West Mountain IPA here won a gold medal at the World Beer Cup and a bronze at the Great American Beer Festival.

2381 Aztec, NE, 505-881-2737, brewery.ilvicino.com

La Cumbre Brewing
The elevated IPA is a crowd favorite here.

3313 Girard Blvd., NE, 505-872-0225, lacumbrebrewing.com

Marble Brewery
Marble took home the coveted Small Brewing Company and Small Brewing Company Brewer of the Year Award at the 2014 Great American Beer Festival, anointing it as one of the nation's best. Two of its beers, the Imperial Red and Double White Ale, also took home gold medals in their respective categories.

111 Marble Ave., NW, 505-243-2739;

5740 Night Whisper, NW, 505-508-4368

marblebrewery.com

Tractor Brewing
The craft creations here have knockout flavors, and the breweries are popular hangouts thanks to the hip vibes and packed community-event schedules.

118 Tulane, SE, 505-443-5654; 1800 Fourth St., NW 505-243-6752, getplowed.com

GRAB A TABLE
ON THE PATIO AT EL PINTO RESTAURANT

Burqueños can debate the best New Mexican food in town until, well, it's time for the next meal. El Pinto is usually in the running, but the restaurant's atmosphere surges to the front of the pack. Here, several patio spaces sprawl beneath hundred-year old cottonwood trees, ristras hang beneath portals, and the strains of mariachi music rise above the conversations shared over margaritas on the rocks. Members of the Thomas family have been serving their family recipes at El Pinto, or "the spot," since 1962, including most recently twin brothers Jim and John, who also began jarring the restaurant's signature salsa. The menu features a full—and tasty—complement of classic New Mexican dishes.

10500 Fourth St., NW, 505-898-1771, elpinto.com

Neighborhood: North Valley

TIP
On Sundays, the restaurant converts its event space into an outdoor yoga studio, where a changing lineup of teachers guide you through a morning vinyasa. Something distracting you during savasana? It's probably the enticing aroma of El Pinto's weekend brunch. Yogis and yoginis receive discount coupons to enjoy the buffet after class.

CYCLE 'ROUND
TO BIKE-IN COFFEE

Albuquerque has a bevy of excellent coffee shops, but none offer the atmosphere of Bike-In Coffee, located at Old Town Farm. Founded in 1977, the twelve-acre farm grows produce, raises chickens for eggs, and produces honey. It welcomes visitors on Saturday and Sunday mornings to a food stand. There's just one catch: you have to arrive under pedal power. To preserve the farm's idyllic setting—and their relationship with neighbors—owners Lanny Tonning and Linda Thorne ask visitors to cycle to the farm on weekends. Bike access is easy. The farm sits in the center of the I-40 bike trail, the Paseo del Bosque Trail, Mountain Road (a Bicycle Boulevard where the speed limit for car traffic is eighteen miles per hour), and sleepy Montoya Street. The hardest choice will be what to choose from the menu: smoothies, soups, salads, savory mini-quiches, or the crowd-pleasing "scookie"—a not-too-sweet, satisfying combination of a scone and a cookie. If you're at the farm on Sundays, you can also point out produce you'd like to take home, farm staff will pick it for you.

949 Montoya St., NW, 505-764-9116, oldtownfarm.com

Neighborhood: Old Town
Kid Friendly

JOIN
THE FOOD TRUCK CARAVAN

Albuquerque is firmly on the food-truck bandwagon. These mobile eateries often show up at local breweries, but to find a particular one, you'll have to check their Facebook pages. Top trucks include Irrational Pie for pizza; Street Food Blvd. for sliders, tacos, and fried cupcakes; Cheesy Street for grilled-cheese sandwiches; and Rustic Food Truck for burgers.

facebook.com/abqfoodtrucks
Kid Friendly

TIP

A changing lineup of food trucks gather for lunch time eats on Tuesdays at Civic Plaza, downtown, and on Wednesdays in the parking lot of Talin Market, in the International District. Both are prime spots to create your own buffet of food truck fare.

MELT FOR THE
CHOCOLATE CARTEL

In the hands of certified master chocolatier and chef Scott J. Van Rixel and brother Tim, chocolate becomes a fine art. Chocolate Cartel creations feature El Rey Venezuelan cacao, which makes up less than ten percent of the beans used worldwide, lending each truffle and bark an exclusive and refined flavor. Although Whole Foods and other major grocers stock Chocolate Cartel creations, visiting the company's Northeast Heights storefront is a trip to the mother ship. Rows of chocolate-covered almonds and toffee salt barks (its top seller) line the walls. Tiers of attractively decorated truffles stack in a glass case. Try the piquant smoked chile, filled with ganache seasoned with red chile, smoked salt, and vanilla, or the espresso, also filled with ganache, this one flavored with espresso from local roaster Moons Coffee & Tea. In recent years, the cartel has expanded its hold on Burqueños' taste buds with a line of gelatos, the most popular of which is the calorie-sin-worthy salted caramel.

315 Juan Tabo Blvd., NE, Ste. A, 505-797-1193, chocolatecartel.com

Neighborhood: Northeast Heights
Kid Friendly

LUNCH AT
THE GROVE CAFÉ & MARKET

This eatery is fresh—from the local, seasonal ingredients, to the bright, light-filled setting. Jason and Lauren Greene have operated the bustling restaurant since 2006, serving salads, sandwiches, and breakfast items made from New Mexican produce, all-natural meats, and artisan breads and cheeses. You'll usually find a long line for this order-at-the-counter café, but you'll never wait long for a table. For lunch, try the Farmers Salad with golden beets, marcona almonds, and goat cheese, or the Turkey Toastie sandwich with Havarti cheese pressed on whole wheat bread. Breakfast is served all day, so don't miss the Grove Pancakes, which are similar to French crêpes topped with fresh fruit, crème fraiche, and local honey, and the pillowy English muffins. Although most customers love the colorful macaroons, for my money, the chocolate walnut cookie with sea salt is the best around.

600 Central Ave., SE, 505-248-9800, thegrovecafemarket.com

Neighborhood: EDo
Kid Friendly

FUN FACT

Breaking Bad fans will remember this eatery as the setting where Walter White—spoiler alert!—laced a packet of Stevia with the poison ricin to kill his former business partner Lydia Rodarte-Quayle (Laura Fraser). The restaurant didn't actually stock the sugar substitute, but since it has received so many requests, you can now find packets on the tables.

DRINK A CUP OF JOE
FROM MICHAEL THOMAS
COFFEE ROASTERS

Albuquerque is flush with neighborhood coffee shops, but this local roaster is one of the best. Michael Thomas roasts all of the fifty varieties it stocks at its original location (in Ridgecrest), and the baristas will give you a free cup of coffee any time you buy a bag of beans to take home. If you're drinking in, dark and light roasts are always freshly brewed, and the specialty espresso drinks (a maple bacon latte, perhaps) are a sweet and savory treat. Plus, owner Michael Sweeney epitomizes Albuquerque's creative ethos: this member of the Air Force dreamed of opening a coffee shop. Now he has two, one of which is just across the street from Kirtland Air Force Base.

111 Carlisle Blvd., SE, 505-255-3330; 202 Bryn Mawr, SE
505-504-7078, michaelthomascoffee.com

Neighborhood: Ridgecrest and Nob Hill

EAT A GREEN-CHILE
SUSHI ROLL

All green, everything. Albuquerqueans will put their beloved chile on and in everything—from pizza to ice cream. (It just makes everything taste better.) This is perhaps never more tested than in the green-chile sushi roll, in which East meets Southwest in the culinary sphere. The chile is usually prepared tempura style, giving the roll a delightful crunch. Azuma Sushi Teppan and Shogun Japanese Restaurant both serve good versions.

Azuma Sushi Teppan
4701 San Mateo Blvd., NE, 505-880-9800, azuma888.com

Neighborhood: Northeast Heights

Shogun Japanese Restaurant
3310 Central Ave., SE, 505-265-9166, on Facebook

Neighborhood: Nob Hill

TIP

For a vegan option, try the Loving Vegan Roll at Loving Vegan. The roll is stuffed with green-chile tempura, avocado, cucumber, vegan lobster, and vegan cream cheese. Then it's deep fried and served with spicy mayo, sriracha, and sweet sauce on top.

3409 Central Ave., NE, 505-890-1555, lovingvegannm.com

MUSIC AND ENTERTAINMENT

GROOVE AT
¡GLOBALQUERQUE!

There are few festivals in the United States where world-music greats such as Calypso Rose and the Afro-Cuban All-Stars play in the same time slot. (Calypso Rose is a prolific writer and songstress, most popularly of calypso music. The Afro-Cuban All Stars recorded the legendary Buena Vista Social Club album and are noted for reviving classic Cuban son music.) These headliners may have hit the stage just one year of the event, but stars such as these are the norm, not the exception, at the two-day festival held each September since 2005. Since that year, ¡Globalquerque! has featured artists from seventy-five countries and across the United States, with ten bands performing per night on three stages. Most play cultural-roots music, often not in English, but that language barrier doesn't keep audiences from dancing in the auditoriums and on the grounds of the National Hispanic Cultural Center, where the celebration is currently held. It's a major regional music fest that's not to be missed.

globalquerque.org

Neighborhood: Barelas

SCREEN A FILM
AT THE KiMo THEATRE

The KiMo Theatre is one of Albuquerque's most prominent architectural landmarks, but it's certainly no relic: The KiMo's schedule is teeming with events. Now an entrant on the National Register of Historic Places, the picture palace and vaudeville theatre opened in 1927. Its architectural style, now known as Pueblo Deco, fused Southwestern and art moderne influences, the latter of which were popular in the 1920s and '30s. Upon its opening, Pablo Abeita, then governor of the Isleta Pueblo, named the theatre using a combination of two Tewa words interpreted as "King of its Kind." The theatre fell into disrepair in the 1960s, but the City of Albuquerque purchased and renovated the structure. The working theatre still screens films today, including such events as the artsy Tim Burton Film Festival and the outdoorsy Reel Rock Film Tour, as well as hosting poetry slams, speakers, and folk music concerts beneath a proscenium arch. The building's distinctive design elements are as well known as what happens on stage: the mezzanine of the lobby features *The Seven Cities of Cibola*, a series of murals by painter Carl von Hassler depicting the mythical cities of gold whose legend initially drew conquistadors into the lands that became New Mexico. Swastikas also appear throughout the theater's décor. Although contemporary audiences may balk at these symbols, when the theater was built, the ancient Native American symbol was used to represent life and prosperity.

421 Central Ave., NW, 505-768-3522, kimotickets.com

Neighborhood: Downtown
Kid Friendly (*depending on the presentation*)

• •

CELEBRATE
FIESTAS DE ALBUQUERQUE

Modern Albuquerque may not look it, but it's in the triple-centenarian club. Established in 1706, the city was named after the Spanish Duke of Alburquerque, thus the city's nickname. The Duke City celebrates its founding each April with—what else?—a party in Old Town, one of its first neighborhoods. The festivities celebrate each of the five phases of the town's history (Native American, Spanish, Mexican, Territorial, and today) with a parade of the founding Spanish families, the swirling skirts of Mexican folkloric dances, and the drumbeat of native dancers. Join in activities such as piñata making or watch blacksmithing demonstrations representing the Territorial Era.

albuquerqueoldtown.com

Neighborhood: Old Town
Kid Friendly

SCREAM FROM THE
STANDS (AND GRASS) AT ISLETA AMPHITHEATRE

This outdoor concert venue has gone by many names, but no matter its appellation, it's the go-to spot in the city for big-name music acts. Everyone from Blake Shelton to John Mayer has played here. Here the cheap seats are the best: Opt for tickets for the grass area so you can watch the coral, orange, and pink hues color the sky at sunset as the opening acts take the stage.

5601 University Blvd., SE, 505-452-5100, isletaamphitheater.net

Neighborhood: Mesa Del Sol

GET PEPPERED
AT THE NATIONAL FIERY FOODS AND BARBECUE SHOW

Some like it hot. Burqueños like their chile scorching. Founded in 1988 by author and chile maven Dave DeWitt, the National Fiery Foods and Barbecue Show is the spiciest show of its kind in the world. During the three-day event in March, more than 200 vendors sponsor booths, most offering tastes of food products. If you want to incite a bout between your taste buds and some of the hottest products on the market—and on the Scoville heat scale—this is your kind of event. The food show also grants Scovie Awards to the best-tasting seasonings, marinades, and condiments. Pick up a program so you can quickly navigate to award-winners such as Lusty Monk Mustards' Original Sin and Scorpion Tail Chili Sauce (the 2014 winner for Hot Sauce, XXX Hot.) The show also includes chef demonstrations from greats who can take—and bring—the heat.

fieryfoodsshow.com

Neighborhood: Northeast Heights

DISCOVER
WHAT THE CHATTER IS ABOUT

French composer Claude Debussy once remarked that "Works of art make rules, rules do not make works of art." Chatter is the rule breaker—and maker—of classical music in Albuquerque. Under the nonprofit umbrella of Ensemble Music New Mexico, Chatter Sunday presents fifty concerts a year featuring both iconic and contemporary classical works, as well as spoken-word poetry at The Kosmos, a stripped-down industrial space where the professionals' musicianship is on full display. David Felberg and friend Eric Walters founded Chatter in 2002 to gain more conducting and composing experience. Chatter merged with Church of Beethoven, which first made Sunday concerts a city tradition, in 2010. Previous concerts have included works by Bach and Chopin, as well as compositions by modern unknowns that challenge the audience members' ears. A couple times a year, favorite local bands such as Le Chat Lunatique, a self-described mangy jazz band, make guest appearances. Speakers including Albuquerque's poet laureates Hakim Bellamy (who served 2012–2014) and Jessica Helen Lopez (who is serving 2014–2016) have graced the stage, as have other notable talents such as Carlos Contreras and Rich Boucher. At The Kosmos, you can also order an espresso and partake of the breakfast pastries Chatter volunteers prepare. Chatter also launches cabaret chamber concerts six times a year and 20-21 performances (bold, large-scale concerts with music from the 20th and 21st centuries) once or twice a year.

Performance Space: 1715 Fifth St., NW
Tickets: chatterabq.org, chatter@chatterabq.org

Neighborhood: Wells Park

SEE A PLAY
AT THE ALBUQUERQUE LITTLE THEATRE

The Albuquerque Little Theatre may be the oldest community theatre group in the city, but its annual season of shows is fresh and lively. The season includes local productions of Broadway theatrical and musical hits, such as *One Flew Over the Cuckoo's Nest* and *Grease*, and productions staged with families in mind, such as *To Kill a Mockingbird*. Founded in 1930, the ALT moved into its current home—designed by renowned architect John Gaw Meem and built by the Works Progress Administration—in 1936. The likes of Vivian Vance, who played Ethel Mertz on *I Love Lucy*, Don Knotts, of *The Andy Griffith Show* and *Three's Company*, and Bill Daily, of *I Dream of Jeannie*, have graced this historic stage.

224 San Pasquale Ave., SW, 505-242-4750, albuquerquelittletheatre.org

Neighborhood: Old Town
Kid Friendly *(depending on the play)*

TIP
To learn more about Albuquerque's more than forty theater venues and companies, visit abqtheatre.org.

FIND A SPOT
IN THE GRASS FOR ZOO MUSIC

Pack a picnic, grab the kids, and throw out a blanket on the lawn at the ABQ BioPark Zoo for this summer music series. The likes of the Indigo Girls and Chris Isaak have played in the band she ll, as have touring acts in pop-rock, Americana, folk, Latin, and jazz. Be sure to arrive early on most Fridays, when the concerts are held, to explore the sixty-four-acre zoo, where more than two hundred animals reside, including quickly growing babies born in the park such as Jazmine the Asian elephant, Abiquiu the giraffe, Pixel the orangutan, and Chopper the white rhino. Many of the animals are active at twilight, occasionally, you'll hear the lions singing backup with roars.

903 10th St., SW, 505-768-2000, cabq.gov

Neighborhood: South Valley
Kid Friendly

RAISE YOUR GLASS
TO THE ALBUQUERQUE WINE FESTIVAL

On Memorial Day Weekend, New Mexico's best vintners descend on Balloon Fiesta Park. Previous years have featured some two-dozen wineries, offering tastes of their best varietals, including Albuquerque area growers such as Matheson Winery, Casa Rondena, and Corrales Winery. The festivities include live music and arts and crafts, but the highlight is, of course, the wine.

abqwinefestival.com

Neighborhood: Northeast Heights

MEET YOUR NEIGHBORS
AT ROUTE 66 SUMMERFEST

There are a few happenings that bring Albuquerqueans out in force—and this block party is one. Nob Hill bustles with food vendors—including a Food Truck Rumble where the mobile eateries battle for the title of Best Street Food—crafts booths, a Cork and Tap garden, and three stages of live music. The event is held on Central Avenue, so of course there's a nod to Route 66 with a classic car show and a "Neon Cruise."

cabq.gov

Neighborhood: Nob Hill
Kid Friendly

CATCH A PERFORMANCE
BY TRICKLOCK COMPANY

Albuquerque's resident theatre company is also one of the city's best exports; it travels internationally to tour works it creates from scratch. The company's home is the Tricklock Performance Laboratory, a black-box space with a fitting name since the company actively develops new plays and workshops them in its Excavations—staged readings of scripts that are then discussed among the audience members and the creators. With a rotating cast of company members, the troupe hosts *The Reptilian Lounge*, the city's longest-running cabaret show featuring poets, musicians, contortionists, and performance artists, to name a few. This company is the mastermind behind Revolutions International Theater Festival, which brings international, cutting-edge theatre to Albuquerque for three weeks each January. Previous years of the festival have featured dance performance pieces from Armenia, a theatrical company from the United Kingdom, and an improv troupe from Austria.

110 Gold Ave., SW, 505-414-3738, tricklock.com

Neighborhood: Downtown

SEE A SHOW
AT POPEJOY HALL

Broadway comes to New Mexico at Popejoy Hall, the biggest indoor performance hall in the state, and an elegant one, too. This University of New Mexico concert venue hosts touring productions of *Wicked*, *Mama Mia*, and other hits. Speakers such as David Sedaris and Ira Glass have graced the stage, as have the Vegas act the Blue Man Group and the Martha Graham Dance Company. This hall, with its sweeping entrance, is made for large-scale productions. Homegrown talent performs here, too, including the New Mexico Philharmonic.

Redondo Drive and Stanford
(at the University of New Mexico Center for the Arts)
505-277-3824, popejoypresents.com
Tickets: unmtickets.com, 505-925-5858

Neighborhood: University
Kid Friendly *(depending on the show)*

LISTEN TO JAZZ AT THE
OUTPOST PERFORMANCE SPACE

This no-frills concert venue is all about the music. Both a nonprofit organization and an intimate performance space, the Outpost presents more than a hundred shows per year. National Endowment for the Arts Jazz Masters—the most prestigious award conferred on such musicians—perform here frequently, including during the summer New Mexico Jazz Festival. (Held in both Santa Fe and Albuquerque, the festival presents its Duke City shows at the Outpost.) Summer also brings an all-local jazz series featuring Dixie to bop. You'll hear other genres here too, including folk, blues, and experimental music. The space may be set up like a jazz lounge or a concert hall. Either way, the one-hundred-sixty-seat house is an intimate venue where you can see musicians at their formidable best.

210 Yale Blvd., SE, 505-268-0044, outpostspace.org

Neighborhood: University

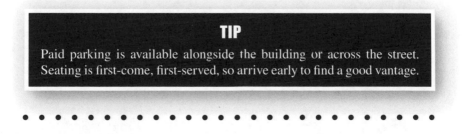

TIP
Paid parking is available alongside the building or across the street. Seating is first-come, first-served, so arrive early to find a good vantage.

EXPLORE
THE UNIVERSITY OF NEW MEXICO
ART MUSEUM

Unless you're a university student, this museum may be off your radar. The two-story annex in the UNM Center for the Arts installs some of the best exhibitions in town. The museum has the 2,400-artworks-strong Raymond Jonson collection, featuring pieces by Jonson, the founder of the Transcendental Painting Group, and many of his contemporaries, including Agnes Martin, Elaine DeKooning, Richard Diebenkorn, and Josef Albers. The museum also hangs a changing series of shows in photography, sculpture, painting, and even significant installations.

Redondo Drive and Stanford
(at the University of New Mexico Center for the Arts)
505-277-4001, unmartmuseum.org

SPORTS AND RECREATION

THRU-BIKE OR HIKE
THE PASEO DEL BOSQUE TRAIL

The Paseo del Bosque Trail has earned a first-place finish in the hearts of Albuquerque's cyclists and runners as the city's premier multi-use path. The sixteen-mile trail runs between the city's north and south edges uninterrupted by car traffic and through the scenic Río Grande bosque. If you complete its entire length, you'll spot elephants, whose ABQ BioPark Zoo enclosure is visible from the path; public art at Tingley Beach, the Rio Grande Valley State Park; privately-owned camels; and Canadian geese at the Valle de Oro National Wildlife Refuge, the city's four-hundred-thirty-acre urban bird sanctuary. There are access points (and often parking areas) at Alameda Boulevard, Paseo del Norte, Montaño Road, Campbell Road, Central Avenue, Marquez Street, and Rio Bravo Boulevard.

cabq.gov

Neighborhood: Citywide
Kid Friendly

PADDLE
THE RÍO GRANDE

Albuquerque and water sports go together like peanut butter and bananas—unexpected, perhaps, but delicious. The Río Grande, the fourth longest river in the United States, cuts a sinuous swath through the heart of the city—much to the delight of paddle-sport enthusiasts. Kayaks and paddleboards, which sit on the surface, fare well in the sometimes-shallow waters that flow through this stretch of river. Coasting along the placid waters, paddlers can see geese, coyotes, and beavers that come to float, drink, and dip in the Río Grande.

Neighborhood: Citywide
Kid Friendly

Outfitters for Tours and Rentals in Albuquerque:
New Mexico Kayak Instruction
505-217-2187, newmexicokayakinstruction.com

Quiet Waters Paddling Adventures
505-771-1234, quietwaterspaddling.com

Southwest Wind Sports
505-350-7942, windsurfnm.com

HIDE BEHIND THE BLINDS
AT THE RIO GRANDE NATURE CENTER STATE PARK

Walking the riverside trails through the cottonwood forests at the Rio Grande Nature Center State Park, you can scarcely tell you're in the heart of a metropolitan area with more than a half-million residents. One of New Mexico's thirty-five state parks, it preserves two hundred seventy acres of cottonwood stands, wetlands, and meadows along the Rio Grande flyway, making it a year-round destination for birders. More than two hundred fifty species have been sighted here, including sandhill cranes, bald eagles, and great blue herons, among others. Duck behind the blinds that border the Candelaria Wetlands and the Discovery Pond outside the visitor center to view the water fowl discretely. Across a footbridge, three easy nature trails await: the Riverwalk Trail, a one-mile loop along the river, the Bosque Loop Trail, a .8-mile trail, and the Aldo Leopold Trail, which is dedicated to the grandfather of the conservation movement and leads to the Aldo Leopold Forest. In winter (when the cottonwood branches are bare) you might spot a porcupine slumbering in the trees. Throughout the year, you may cross paths with beavers, cottontail rabbits, or coyotes.

2901 Candelaria, NW, 505-344-7240, rgnc.org, nmparks.com

Neighborhood: North Valley
Kid Friendly

TIP

The volunteer organization Friends of the Rio Grande Nature Center offers guided, weekend bird walks, nature walks, and monthly twilight hikes. Check the schedule online to join in.

WALK THE WIDE OPEN
(SPACE)

There isn't just wide-open space around Albuquerque, there's wide-open space within the city. In fact, Albuquerque has more parkland per capita than any city within the United States (a total of more than twenty-seven thousand acres via twenty-seven city-owned tracts). The Open Space Visitor Center is a fitting jumping-off point for your explorations. The center has interpretive exhibits, an art gallery, and agricultural fields that draw an array of wildlife. (For the athletically inclined, there's also a weekend yoga class held at the center. Depending on the season, it may be held inside or out, but it's always held within epic views of the Sandia Mountains or the gardens.) To get out on the trails, locals favor Elena Gallegos Picnic Area and Albert G. Simms Park, in the foothills of the Sandia Mountains. A network of paths loops through the six-hundred-forty-acre park, wending through stands of piñon and juniper, and unfolding into views of the Sandias (to the east), Mount Taylor (to the west), and the Jemez Mountains (to the north). From here, the Pino Trail extends into the Sandia Mountain Wilderness and, via a climb, to the Crest Trail that follows the top of the city's iconic mountains.

Visitor Center: 6500 Coors, NW, 505-897-8831, cabq.gov

Neighborhood: Citywide
Kid Friendly

RIDE OVER
TO A RODEO

You'll be hootin' and hollerin' for the cowboys and cowgirls who compete in traditional rodeo sports, including tie-down roping, team roping, steer wrestling, bronc and bull riding, and barrel racing. The Professional Rodeo Cowboys Association (PRCA) hosts competitions through out September's New Mexico State Fair, at Expo New Mexico, and each spring, when Professional Bull Riders face off at the Ty Murray Invitational.

exponm.com/state-fair, pbr.com

Neighborhood: Citywide
Kid Friendly

DRESS UP
FOR DAY OF THE TREAD

Day of the Tread is the definitive answer to the question, "Where can I bike next to a banana and run with the Hulk?" This annual athletic event, held in October, draws its name from the Day of the Dead, and gives each of its races a Halloween twist by inviting participants to dress up in costumes. The races include 100-, 80-, 64-, 26-, and 11-mile bike rides, and a half-marathon, 10K, 5K, one-mile, and kid's K runs.

dayofthetread.com

Neighborhood: Citywide
Kid Friendly

TIP
The Duke City Marathon (dukecitymarathon.com) is the city's top running event, in which racers compete sans costumes. The Albuquerque Tour de Cure, hosted by the American Diabetes Association, offers long rides also without the banana-costume factor.

REJUVENATE
AT TAMAYA MIST SPA & SALON

File Tamaya under places that make you go, "Ooh." This resort, co-owned by Hyatt and the Pueblo of Santa Ana, nestles in the Río Grande bosque. It offers plush accommodations, dining at the Corn Maiden restaurant, and golf at Twin Warriors. All are decadent, but none as much as the spa, where the surrounding land and native peoples inspire its signature treatments. The Three Sisters Salt Scrub blends blue-corn meal, Anasazi bean, pumpkin seeds (all traditional Puebloan foods) and salts to exfoliate your skin. Combine that with the Prickly Pear Toning Treatment to moisturize, firm, and tone your whole body.

1300 Tuyuna Trail, 505-867-1234, tamaya.hyatt.com

Neighborhood: Bernalillo

HIKE
LA LUZ TRAIL

Trekking La Luz Trail is a rite of passage for Albuquerqueans. The eight-mile trail (one way) climbs four thousand feet along its route from the foothills to the crest of the Sandia Mountains. Switchbacks will help you manage the steepness as the trail rises through piñon/juniper-dotted foothills to ponderosa forests. The views of the city and the Río Grande Valley below are worth the sweat. Once you've summited, you can descend the way you came or head over to the Sandia Peak Tramway departure area to glide back to the base (which will drop you off in a different parking lot than the one you started in). Please note: this is a strenuous trail that should only be attempted by those with the physical fitness to accomplish the hike. Visitors should take note that the trail's altitude ranges from seven thousand to more than ten thousand feet. Don't make the Albuquerque Mountain Rescue Council save the day because you've underestimated the trail's difficulty!

Neighborhood: Northeast Heights

Cibola National Forest Sandia Ranger Station
505-281-3304, fs.usda.gov/cibola

TIP
If you're a trail-running superstar, enter the lottery for a spot in the La Luz Trail Run. The Albuquerque Road Runners club sponsors this race each August. abqroadrunners.com

PACK
THE PIT

Albuquerque may be short on professional sports teams, but it's long on school pride for the University of New Mexico Lobos. Cherry-and-silver-clad basketball fans are particularly zealous when they fill every seat in the university's arena, nicknamed "The Pit" because its playing floor lies thirty-seven feet below street level. The Pit has a reputation as being one of the loudest venues in college basketball and a winning one—at least for the Lobos, who have won more than eighty percent of their games on their home court. The Pit has also hosted NCAA tournament games. In 2010, it was renovated, and, in 2014, it received a fresh name: WisePies Arena a.k.a. The Pit. But to Burqueños, it will always be simply The Pit. Just remember: in this arena, everyone's a Lobo. Woof, woof, woof.

1111 University Blvd., SE, golobos.com
Tickets: (877) 664-8661, unmtickets.com

Neighborhood: University
Kid Friendly

GET KNOCKED OUT
WITH MIXED-MARTIAL ARTS

Albuquerque has emerged as the clear winner in the cage match for the country's top mixed-martial arts training destination. Coach Greg Jackson's training curriculum and eponymous Jackson's Martial Arts & Fitness Academy churn out UFC champions, including Albuquerque native Carlos Condit (who has held the title in the welterweight division) and transplant Jon "Bones" Jones (the light heavyweight champion) to name two. More than sixty professional fighters train there, and the public can join submission fighting training classes, too. If you want to watch rather than compete in the octagon, Isleta Resort and Casino hosts matches in Jackson's MMA series.

Train: 2801 Eubank Blvd., SE
505-881-7911, jacksonsmartialartsandfitness.com

Neighborhood: Northeast Heights

Watch: Isleta Resort and Casino
11000 Broadway, SE, 505-724-3800, isleta.com

Neighborhood: South Valley

TRACE THE PAST
AT PETROGLYPH NATIONAL MONUMENT

Native Americans and Spanish settlers who have lived in the Río Grande Valley have left indelible cultural influences, and they've left physical traces, too: in the black volcanic rocks of the Petroglyph National Monument, one of the largest such sites in North America. The monument, on the city's west mesa, protects more than seven thousand acres of land, which is dotted with these 400- to 700-year-old markings. Boca Negra Canyon features three self-guided trails offering views of some two hundred markings of birds, snakes, spirals, geographic designs, and handprints. The more rugged, 2.2-mile Rinconada Canyon Trail offers views of some four hundred petroglyphs, as well as of the volcanic eruption and formations that created the landscape there.

Intersection of Western Trail and Unser Blvd., NW
505-899-0205, nps.gov/petr

Neighborhood: Westside
Kid Friendly

SOAK
AT BETTY'S BATH AND DAY SPA

Betty's Bath and Day Spa lives up to the mission owner Elissa Breitbard established when it opened in 2000: to be a relaxation and wellness retreat. The spa offers coed communal, women-only, and private soaking pools. Adobe walls and shade trees enclose the pools, giving them a far-away feel, though the spa is set in the heart of the city. Betty's prides itself on having the best massage therapists in town and lives up to its promise with deep-tissue, sports, pregnancy, Thai, and sinus-relief options. To maximize your experience, soak prior to a massage. Betty's signature spa treatment is the "Dulce de Cuerpo," a full-body exfoliating treatment that begins with a soothing coconut-oil treatment, followed by hand and foot massages, then the namesake sugar scrub.

1835 Candelaria, NW, 505-341-3456, bettysbath.com

Neighborhood: North Valley

GLIDE ALONG
THE SANDIA PEAK TRAMWAY

If Albuquerque had an Empire State Building equivalent, this is it. The tram is easily the largest tourist attraction in the city and offers spectacular views of the city and Río Grande Valley during the 2.7-mile ride from the foothills to the crest of the Sandia Mountains. At one point during the trip, the car hangs some one thousand feet above Big Canyon, at approximately the same height above the ground as the top of the Empire State Building. In 1966, the tram made its first voyage as a way to transport passengers quickly to the backside of the mountain, home to the Sandia Peak Ski area. (The tram receives regular maintenance and safety testing, not to worry.) The cables for the tram pass through only two towers on the way to the top, the car dips and swings slightly after passing through each, usually eliciting a few gasps from passengers. The tram glides smoothly above granite rock faces, pinnacles, and spires, offering occasional views of black bears, mountain lions, and mule deer below. Astute observers may even spot the wreckage of TWA Flight 260, which crashed into the mountains on February 19, 1955. At the summit, first catch your breath: You're standing at 10,378 feet in elevation. Then, take in the eleven thousand square miles of views possible from this vantage, including those of Mount Taylor, Cabezon, and the Jemez Mountains. Some passengers enjoy meals at High Finance Restaurant, and many follow the Crest Trail through the ponderosa pine forests either north or south. For many hikers, the Kiwanis rock cabin, 1.5 miles along the north Crest Trail is both destination and turn-around-point. During summer, chairlifts offer scenic rides down the east side of the mountain—as well as lifts for mountain bikers who choose to zoom down that hillside and want to hitch a ride back up.

30 Tramway Rd., NE, 505-856-7325, sandiapeak.com
Neighborhood: Northeast Heights
Kid Friendly

SHRED
AT SANDIA PEAK SKI AREA

Sandia Peak Ski Area is the closest ski area to the city. Via the Sandia Peak Tramway, skiers can be on the slopes within fifteen minutes of the western base. Most, however, choose to drive to the Double Eagle Day Lodge where a café, sports shop, and ski school await. The ski area receives an average of one hundred twenty-five inches of snow each year. Thirty runs are accessible via five lifts, with more than half of the terrain suiting intermediate skiers. Opening and closing dates depend on snowfall, but the season generally runs from late December through mid-March.

From Albuquerque, take I-40 east to Cedar Crest. At exit 175, head north on NM 14 to the Crest Scenic Byway 536. Follow the byway six miles to the ski area. 505-242-9052, sandiapeak.com

Neighborhood: East Mountains
Kid Friendly

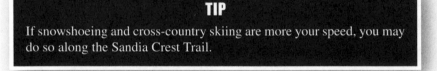

TIP
If snowshoeing and cross-country skiing are more your speed, you may do so along the Sandia Crest Trail.

ROOT FOR THE
ALBUQUERQUE ISOTOPES

For professional sports in Albuquerque, head to Isotopes Park to watch the town's AAA baseball team, which has made its home in the city since 2003. Since 2014, the Isotopes have been a minor-league farm team for the Colorado Rockies. (The team was previously affiliated with other franchises.) An episode of *The Simpsons*, in which Homer protests the Springfield Isotopes' plans to move to Albuquerque by going on a hunger strike, inspired the team's name. The name fits, thanks to Albuquerque's connection to nuclear history. Orbit, the mascot, seems to have experienced some radiation: It's unclear if he's an alien, a dog, a bear, or all three. Regardless, he's quite friendly—and flexible. He joins Albuquerque yogis and yoginis each spring for a day of yoga at the park. During the season, there isn't a bad seat in the stadium. For cheap seats, opt for the lawn. Families with kids should head to the Fun Zone for rides and games. Check the schedule for games offering fireworks and other giveaways. A note about the park dress code: Yes, Isotopes gear is in vogue, but so is Albuquerque Dukes gear. The Dukes were the city's team until 2000, and Burqueños still proudly wear the logo.

1601 Avenida Cesar Chavez, SE, 505-222–4058, abqisotopes.com

Neighborhood: University
Kid Friendly

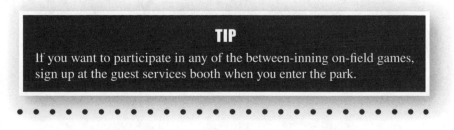

TIP
If you want to participate in any of the between-inning on-field games, sign up at the guest services booth when you enter the park.

FISH
AT SHADY LAKES

High summer, there are few cooler places in the city than beneath the cottonwoods along the shores of Shady Lakes' ponds. This family-friendly fishing destination stocks trout, bass, catfish, and bluegill and gives the chance for kids to cast without the need of licenses.

11033 Fourth St., NW/NM 313, NW, 505-898-2568, shadylakes.com

Neighborhood: North Valley
Kid Friendly

DOWN TO THE FISHING HOLE

You can also fish from dawn 'til dusk at Tingley Beach, a part of the ABQ BioPark. Admission is free, but anglers older than 12 years need a valid New Mexico fishing license.

1800 Tingley Dr., SW, 505-768-2000, cabq.gov

SOAK
IN THE JEMEZ MOUNTAINS

Getting to the village of Jemez Springs, sixty miles northwest of Albuquerque, is half the fun: You'll drive the Jemez Mountain trail, a National Scenic Byway that traces the Jemez River past red rocks and sheer canyon cliffs into the Jemez Mountains. In town, you can dip into healing mineral waters at the Jemez Springs Bath House or Giggling Springs, but most outdoor adventurers crave the outdoor surroundings of the natural hot springs here. There are two popular treks: From the Battleship Rock parking lot, a 3.5-mile hike (round-trip) leads to the McCauley Hot Springs, where warm waters will soothe any time of year. North of Jemez Springs, off NM 4, a short trail leads to the river and up to the smaller Spence Hot Springs, which keeps a constant temperature of ninety-five degrees. If you're in the market for a day hike sans soak, a 2.8-mile loop trail along the East Fork of the Jemez Trail is a lovely walk.

Sixty miles north of Albuquerque, off NM 4, jemezsprings.org

Neighborhood: Jemez Springs
Kid Friendly

Jemez Springs Bath House, 62 Jemez Springs Plaza
(575) 829-3303, jemezsprings.org

Giggling Springs Hot Springs, 40 Abouselman Loop
(575) 829-9175, gigglingsprings.com

CYCLE
A BICYCLE BOULEVARD

Bicycling Magazine named Albuquerque one of the most bike-friendly cities in the United States, and it's a well-deserved accolade. More than four hundred miles of paths—including multi-use trails, streets with bike lanes, and bicycle-only routes—can get you nearly any place you'd like to go. The City of Albuquerque even designated several Bicycle Boulevards down Silver, 14th Street, and Mountain, slowing the car traffic to eighteen miles per hour to make these routes more hospitable to cyclists. These expressways are marked with purple signs and offer scenic riding routes through the urban landscape.

cabq.gov

Neighborhood: Citywide
Kid Friendly

HIKE KASHA-KATUWE
TENT ROCKS NATIONAL MONUMENT

The distinct volcanic formations here can be seen only one other place in the world (in Cappadocia, Turkey), and they're in the Duke City's backyard. "Kasha-Katuwe" means "white cliffs" in the traditional Kcresan language of the nearby Cochiti Pueblo, but white is just one hue of the colorful cliffs and hoodoos at this national monument. The 1.2-mile, easy Cave Loop Trail wanders among the pumice and tuff pinnacles, some of which tower ninety feet, the 1.5-mile Canyon Trail treks up a narrow canyon to a mesa top offering views of the Sangre de Cristo, Jemez, and Sandia Mountains. In the arroyos, you may spot translucent obsidian (volcanic glass) orbs, another testament to the monument's geological past.

Fifty-five miles northeast of Albuquerque, off Indian Service Route 92
505-331-6259, blm.gov

Neighborhood: Cochiti
Kid Friendly

SETTLE INTO A LOW GEAR
FOR MOUNTAIN BIKING

New Mexico is fast becoming a top destination for fat-tire fanatics, but Albuquerqueans needn't go far to find some of the state's best trails. In the foothills, the Manzano/Four Hills, Elena Gallegos (especially along the 365 Trail), and Bear Canyon Open Spaces are all local favorites. All of the trails offer mostly dirt single track, with some sections of loose gravel and steep drops, and enough boulder sections to test your technical mettle. On the east side of the mountains, there are more grueling climbs—and rapid descents—on the steep Sandia Peak Ski Area trails, including King of the Mountain, the North and South Faulty Trails, and lower loops along trails such as Medio.

mtbproject.com

Neighborhood: Foothills and East Mountains
Kid Friendly

WATCH THE
SANDIA MOUNTAINS TURN PINK

When the sun sets over Albuquerque, it's difficult to decide where to look: to the multi-hued west where the sun dips below the horizon, or to the east, to see the Sandia Mountains in alpenglow. Light glinting off potassium-feldspar in the granite mountains gives the hills their distinctive—though not namesake—watermelon hue. (Sandía means "watermelon" in Spanish.) One of the best places to watch the sunset is from the Volcanoes Day Use Area, part of Petroglyph National Monument. There you can hike loop trails up the three sister volcanoes that dot the western mesa (JA, Black, and Vulcan), each offering spectacular city and mountain views.

Off Atrisco Vista Blvd., 505-899-0205, nps.gov/petr

Neighborhood: Westside
Kid Friendly

TIP

If you plan to watch the sunset from the Volcanoes Day Use Area, be sure to leave your car outside the park gates. The parking lot is closed—and the gate locked—promptly at 5 p.m.

TAKE AN OTHERWORLDLY WALK
AT OJITO WILDERNESS AREA

One of the three wilderness areas in Albuquerque's immediate orbit, Ojito is perhaps the hardest to love. Badlands, steep mesas, and box canyons make up the landscape here—quite austere compared to the forested surroundings at Sandia and the wildlife bonanza at Bosque Del Apache. However, the bands of rust, ochre, and alabaster shale make this eleven-thousand-acre landscape imminently tantalizing. Follow two trails for your explorations: The Seismosaurus Trail through arroyos and across mesa tops for views, and the Hoodoo Trail, which wends among marbled pinnacles.

Sixty miles northwest of Albuquerque, off US 550
505-761-8700, blm.gov

Neighborhood: Outside of Bernalillo
Kid Friendly

TIP

Getting to the wilderness area trails requires travel down maintained dirt roads. Mechanized travel, including by bicycle, isn't permitted within the wilderness area.

CULTURE AND
HISTORY

GRAB A SEAT
AT THE GATHERING OF NATIONS POWWOW

During the grand entry to this competition powwow each April, a drumbeat announces the presence of three thousand indigenous people streaming into The Pit. The singers' voices rise above even the jingling, pounding footsteps of the dancers who swirl in their colorful, traditional regalia. Participants, who hail from some fifty tribes in the United States, Canada, and Mexico preserve their traditional cultures and share it with attendees. The powwow also includes the Miss Indian World pageant and an Indian Traders Market, where you'll find everything from cone jingles for fancy dance dresses to Navajo jewelry. Traditional and contemporary native musicians play at Stage 49, with groups ranging from rock to hip-hop.

1111 University Blvd., SE, gatheringofnations.com

Neighborhood: University

DANCE OVER
TO THE FESTIVAL FLAMENCO
INTERNACIONAL DE ALBURQUERQUE

Flamenco may be a step toward the city's Spanish roots, but in Albuquerque the dramatic dance form has its own distinctive flare. This weeklong festival held each June is regarded as the longest-standing flamenco event outside of Spain. Because it unites dancers and musicians from all over the world, it's also one of the most notable. You can catch a performance by the changing list of world-renowned featured artists—traditionally at the University of New Mexico's Rodey Theatre and National Hispanic Cultural Center's Albuquerque Journal Theatre—or try your hands at the castanets and feet at the passionate dance in classes.

nationalinstituteofflamenco.org

Neighborhood: University and Barelas

TIP
Year-round, to see this dance form, look for performances by Yjastros, the American flamenco repertory company headquartered in Albuquerque.

WATCH
A MATACHINES DANCE

Watching a Matachines dance is an only-in-New Mexico experience. (Although the dance is performed other places, the state's villages and tribes have given it their own unique twists.) The masked dance tells the story of conquest. The characters include a monarch, masked captains, La Malinche (an Indian woman who had a relationship with Hernán Cortés), El Toro (the bull, who may also symbolize the Devil depending on the interpretation), and the Abuelo (grandfather) and Abuela (grandmother). Around Albuquerque, you can see the traditional dance performed each August as part of the festivities at Las Fiestas de San Lorenzo in Bernalillo and each January 1 at Jemez Pueblo, both north of Albuquerque. Jemez Pueblo performs both the Hispanic and Native American versions of the dance, for which participants wear different regalia and tell slightly different versions of the story.

townofbernalillo.org, jemezpueblo.org

Neighborhood: Bernalillo and Jemez Pueblo

BROWSE THE NATIONAL
HISPANIC CULTURAL CENTER

This world-class center is a one-stop shop to explore several facets of culture. Its visual art collection is a standout: the eleven-thousand-square-foot gallery space exhibits exciting contemporary and traditional works from renowned Latin American, Spanish, and Nuevo Mexicano artists, such as Charles M. Carrillo and Luis Jimenez, as well as changing exhibits on photography, tapas (small bites of Spanish cuisine), and *papel picado* (perforated paper). The center also stages music and dance performances, offers dance and cooking classes, and operates a restaurant.

1701 Fourth St., SW, 505-246-2261, nationalhispaniccenter.org

Neighborhood: Barelas

TIP
Plan your visit around visiting the Torreón (watchtower) at the entrance. Inside, Mundos de Mestizaje retells three thousand years of Hispanic history and has earned acclaim as the largest concave fresco in North America. The true fresco by Santa Fe artist Frederico Vigil took more than ten years to design and paint, Vigil used local models for his depictions of Toltecs, Mayans, medieval Spanish, and early Albuquerqueans, all of whom figure in the painting.

VIEW THE SQUARE KIVA
AT CORONADO HISTORIC SITE

This kiva (ceremonial chamber) doubles up on exceptionalities: It's square, rather than round. And it was once home to some of the finest examples of pre-Columbian art found in the United States, which were painted as frescos in the fifteenth century. The monument is named for Francisco Vasquez de Coronado, whose entrada camped near Kuaua Pueblo (meaning "evergreen" in the Tiwa language) between 1540 and 1542. Archeologists from the Museum of New Mexico excavated the Pueblo remains in the 1930s, unearthing the murals, which they painstakingly removed. You can see fourteen sections of the original murals in the visitors' center. With a guide or ranger escort, you can visit the square kiva, where Ma Pe Wi, a Zia Pueblo artist, recreated the murals there in 1938 and which were restored in 2013. The frescos depict soaring eagles and swallows, seeds, and life-giving raindrops.

485 Kuaua Rd., 505-867-5351, nmhistoricsites.org

Neighborhood: Bernalillo
Kid Friendly

SIT BACK
FOR *FIRST FRIDAY FRACTALS*

Your inner nerd can have a night out on the town at *First Friday Fractals*, a monthly show during which fractals swirl across the full dome of the planetarium at the New Mexico Museum of Natural History & Science. Fractals, both a natural and mathematical phenomenon, are repeating patterns that display at every scale, and these designs come to life in the IMAX-style presentation. The first show features original music and narration that describes the phenomenon. A second show, played at two later showings, *Fractals Rock!*, offers a similar immersive journey with less explanation.

1801 Mountain Rd., NW, 505-841-2800, nmnaturalhistory.org

Neighborhood: Old Town
Kid Friendly

TIP
Buy your tickets in advance as these shows always sell out. Online ticket sales end at noon on the day of the show.

FLY HIGH
AT THE ALBUQUERQUE
INTERNATIONAL BALLOON FIESTA

The Albuquerque International Balloon Fiesta is the city's largest sporting event and its most popular festival rolled into one. AIBF is also the largest gathering of balloons and balloonists in the world. In 2011, with three hundred forty-five balloons taking flight, the AIBF set the record for the most balloons lifting off in an hour, usually, more than five hundred hot-air balloon teams attend each year. The nine-day event, which is held annually the first week of October, features a variety of events throughout the week. The most popular are the morning mass ascensions, when attendees huddle in the dawn light—hot chocolate and breakfast burritos in hand—watching the balloons inflate and take off from Balloon Fiesta Park. The afternoon special shapes rodeos, with balloons in the forms of Yoda, Darth Vader, and others, are also favorites. During evening glows, balloons are tethered to the ground and fire their burners to light up the night sky.

5000 Balloon Fiesta Pkwy., NE, (888) 422-7277, 505-821-1000
balloonfiesta.com

Neighborhood: Northeast Heights
Kid Friendly

● ●

TIPS

Although there's parking available at the field, the best way to visit is via the Park and Ride shuttle buses from satellite locations around the city.

Balloons Are Always in Burque: The Anderson-Abruzzo Albuquerque International Balloon Museum is open year-round, telling the history of the sport both around the globe and in town. Most enthralling are the original and replica versions of historic crafts, including the Double Eagle II, in which Albuquerque balloonists Maxie Anderson and Ben Abruzzo, along with Larry Newman, completed the first manned crossing of the Atlantic Ocean in 1978. During the fiesta, you can attend the Diamond Club, which offers a VIP-all-the-way experience with a breakfast buffet and viewing of the field from the museum's balcony. Rainbow Ryders is a top company for balloon rides. It flies year-round (weather permitting).

9201 Balloon Museum Dr., NE, 505-768-6020
balloonmuseum.com

5601 Eagle Rock Ave., NE, (800) 725-2477
rainbowryders.com

GALLERY HOP
AT FIRST FRIDAY ARTScrawl

2015 marks twenty-five years of ARTScrawls in Albuquerque. A citywide, self-guided gallery tour happens each first Friday. Participating galleries usually mark the occasion with new exhibitions and artist receptions, but check the schedule online for details about specific shows. The galleries range from those presenting thought-provoking, contemporary creations, such as 516 Arts, to those with more traditional fine art, such as Sumner & Dene.

artscrawlabq.org

Neighborhood: Citywide

WALK THE AISLES
OF WEEMS INTERNATIONAL ART FEST

Weems is the cream that rises to the top of Albuquerque's many art markets. Since it began in 1982, this November tradition at Expo New Mexico has become one of the largest and most prestigious art events in the state. Jurors select two hundred eighty artists for the show, meaning all are at the top of their respective mediums. Throughout the year, you can find much of the local artists' work at Weems Galleries and Framing, the organizing gallery.

Expo New Mexico: 300 San Pedro Dr., NE
weemsinternationalartfest.org

Neighborhood: International District

TAKE A PUBLIC
ART WALK

Albuquerque boasts one of the oldest public art programs in the country. In 1978, voters passed the one percent for the arts initiative, which has erected some eight hundred works, including four hundred sculptures, murals, paintings, and mosaics in downtown alone. The Albuquerque Convention Center has a large collection of pieces within the building and, on the exterior, students from the Mayor's Art Summer Institute at Harwood Art Center have created a mosaic over the course of more than a decade that tells the story of New Mexico's cultural history. Don't miss the following installations, which demonstrate the breadth of the collection: *Sidewalk Society*, by Glenna Goodacre, a collection of bronze statues at Third and Tijeras; *La Pared de Imágenes* (The Wall of Images) by Byron Wickstrom, featuring forty-two individual metal sculptures, each with a distinct geometric form and patina; and *Auto Hawk*, by Christopher Fennell, a twenty-four-foot-tall sculpture incorporating thirty car doors on Second Street. Find suggested tours and information about the individual works on the City of Albuquerque's website.

cabq.gov

Neighborhood: Citywide
Kid Friendly

PHOTO OP

The *Chevy on a Stick* (formerly known as Cruising San Mateo I by Barbara Grygutis before it earned its nickname in the early 1990s) is one of the city's most notable—and most controversial—public art pieces. The sculpture, in which a full-sized, tiled car sits atop an arch, has become a must-do photo op.

FLY AWAY
TO THE SPACESHIP HOUSE

Ok, that's not the house's proper name. But that's what Burqueños call Bart Prince's residence and studio. Built 1983–84, this structure and its companion, also from the famed architect's portfolio, certainly look as though they flew right out of a sci-fi movie and into an Albuquerque residential neighborhood. Prince, who is known for pushing design boundaries, works in the cylindrical studio at the front of the property just behind the earth berm. He designed the second (submarine-shaped) story to be heated via passive solar. The stone tower at the south end of the property was added in 1990 and serves as a library and storage area.

3501 and 3507 Monte Vista Blvd.

Neighborhood: Nob Hill

ALTERNATE BART PRINCE ARCHITECTURE SIGHTING
Bart Prince also designed the swirling spiral building, similar to that of a snail shell, at the entrance of Casas de Suenos (casasdesuenos.com), a bed and breakfast in Old Town.

SEE AN INDIE FLICK
AT THE GUILD

The Guild is Albuquerque's independent film house. It screens all manner of low-budget and off-the-radar films, from classic cult hits to newly produced film-festival darlings. Oscar-nominated shorts (animated, documentary, and live action) and full-length documentaries get their day on the big screen here during awards season. The Guild is also the home of the Sin Fronteras Film Festival, a Latin American Film Festival, and the New Mexico Italian Film Festival. The intimate house has only a few dozen seats, so arrive early to find one and get your popcorn. Don't miss the red-chile powder topping.

3405 Central Ave., NE, 505-255-1848, guildcinema.com

Neighborhood: Nob Hill

GET YOUR FACE PAINTED
FOR THE DÍA DE LOS MUERTOS Y MARIGOLDS PARADE

Sugar skull art comes to life on the faces of the participants of the Día de Los Muertos y Marigolds Parade. Held in honor of the Mexican holiday Día de Los Muertos, the parade through the South Valley features throngs of walkers and cars—from low riders to hearses—decked out in honor of the dead. Garlands of flowers, real and fabric, string across mock coffins and headstones, and puppeteers make eight-foot-tall skeletons dance to the trumpets of mariachi music. The aroma of marigold flowers rises as parade participants sprinkle the golden petals as they walk. Everyone is welcome to participate (with an application), or you can just watch. The parade funnels into a park where altars pay homage to friends and family members who have passed.

muertosymarigolds.org

Neighborhood: South Valley
Kid Friendly

EARN A CERTIFICATE
OF BRAVERY AT THE AMERICAN
INTERNATIONAL RATTLESNAKE MUSEUM

To earn your certificate of bravery here, you'll have to navigate an expansive collection of live rattlesnakes—a larger collection than even the likes of the National or the San Diego zoos. Chihuahuan ridge-nose, canebrake, and tiger rattlesnakes are all on display in this conservation-minded center, as is snake memorabilia.

202 San Felipe St., NW, 505-242-6569, rattlesnakes.com

Neighborhood: Old Town
Kid Friendly

TOUR *BREAKING BAD*
FILMING LOCATIONS

Breaking Bad, the TV drama that put Albuquerque on the pop-culture map, had locals asking if the show about a teacher-turned-meth-cook made the city look badass—or just bad. Either way, the show, which was both filmed and set in the Duke City, has attracted legions of fans on pilgrimages to visit the real-life locations that turned up on the AMC drama. For a self-guided tour, see the following list of must-see filming locations. For a *Breaking Bad* experience through and through, hitch a ride on a *Breaking Bad* RV Tour. Actors and extras from the show lead the tours on one of the three 1986 Fleetwood Bounder RVs that appeared on the small screen. The ringing of Hector Salamanca's bell (a look-alike) marks the tour's departure to seventeen of the show's filming locations, including Tuco's office (on the second floor of real-life Java Joe's), Combo's corner (at Second Street and Hazeldine), the DEA offices (the agency's true-to-life whereabouts), and other must-see locations.

breakingbadrvtours.com

Neighborhood: Citywide

MUST-SEE FILMING LOCATIONS

Crossroads Motel
Northeast corner of Central Ave., SE
and Oak St., NE

Dog House Drive-In
1216 Central Ave., NW

Jesse's House*
Northeast corner of Los Alamos Avenue
and 16th St., SW

Mister Car Wash a.k.a. A1A Car Wash
9516 Snow Heights Cir., NE

Twisters a.k.a. Los Pollos Hermanos
4257 Isleta Blvd., SW

Walt's House*
3828 Piermont Dr., NE
(Intersection of Piermont Drive and Orlando Place)

*Please note: these are private residences. Stay on the sidewalk
and be respectful of the owners' wishes and privacy.

WATCH A TRADITIONAL DANCE
AT THE INDIAN PUEBLO CULTURAL CENTER

In New Mexico, traditional Native American dances, which have deep cultural roots in each Pueblo and tribe, are reflections of yesteryear and today. Usually seeing such dances requires a road trip. It's well worth the drive, but in town, you can head to the Indian Pueblo Cultural Center where groups from different Pueblos and tribes share traditional steps each weekend—and more often during peak times, such as during the Albuquerque International Balloon Fiesta. You may encounter the Olla Maidens from Zuni Pueblo, the Red Turtle Dancers from Pojoaque Pueblo, or buffalo dancers from Jemez Pueblo. Through dance, each of the state's nineteen Pueblos shares its distinctive rituals, regalia, and culture. The IPCC's museum, gift shop, and Pueblo Harvest Café—serving traditional native foods both down-home and upscale—are also worth exploring.

2401 12th St., NW, 505-843-7270, indianpueblo.org

Neighborhood: North Valley
Kid Friendly

TIP

During summer, the IPCC's Party on the Patio each Friday, with cocktails, a buffet, and live music, is one of the busiest—and most enjoyable—happy hours in town.

VISIT THE PAST
AT THE ALBUQUERQUE MUSEUM
OF ART AND HISTORY

With the *Only in Albuquerque* history gallery, this gem is a repository of the city's past. The exhibit tells the story of the Río Grande Valley. The displays show Navajo and Pueblo blankets (both historical and artistic artifacts), farm and ranch tools, and early European maps of New Spain. The museum's collection of helmets, swords, and Colonial European armor is considered among the best in the United States. On Albuquerque's fertile creative grounds, history is woven with art. The creatives featured in the museum's permanent art exhibit, *Common Ground: Art in New Mexico*, reads like a who's who list of southwest art: it features the works of Ernest L. Blumenschein, Georgia O'Keeffe, and Fritz Scholder, to name a few.

2000 Mountain Road, NW, 505-243-7255, albuquerquemuseum.org

Neighborhood: Old Town
Kid Friendly

TIP

The museum offers free admission several times each month: every Sunday morning, from 9 a.m. to 1 p.m., the first Wednesday of the month, from 9 a.m. to 5 p.m., and the third Thursday of the month, from 5 to 8 p.m. The third Thursday events feature special programming (think: Geeks Who Drink quizzes), and a light menu and cash bar at the museum café.

TUNE IN

The New Mexico Jazz Workshop teams with the museum each summer for Salsa, and Jazz & Blues Under the Stars with concerts (usually Friday and Saturday nights) in the outdoor amphitheater.
nmjazz.org

GET GLOWING
WITH LUMINARIAS IN OLD TOWN

Duke City denizens' favorite holiday tradition is seeing luminarias on Christmas Eve. These decorations may be modest (just paper bags weighted down with sand and a small candle lit inside), but the ethereal flickering of thousands makes the holiday merry and bright. The best neighborhoods to see them are Old Town and the Country Club, where businesses and residences line adobe walls and walkways with the lanterns. For the holiday, the City of Albuquerque turns its public buses into tour coaches to drive passengers through these renowned neighborhoods to see the lights while staying warm. Tickets for the tours sell out early—sometimes in one day. To ensure you get one, buy yours the day after Thanksgiving, when they go on sale. If you want to walk rather than ride, visit Old Town after 9 p.m. (my favorite time) when the crowds, cars, and buses have dissipated.

Luminaria Tour: cabq.gov

Neighborhood: Old Town and Country Club
Kid Friendly

DICTION DEBATE

Albuquerqueans refer to the bagged beauties as luminarias. However, in northern New Mexico, paper bags with a candle inside are called farolitos and small bonfires luminarias. Who's right? Whomever you're speaking to at the time.

GLOW UPSIZED

On Christmas Eve, a dozen pilots tether their hot-air balloons at Arroyo Del Oso Golf Course, in the Northeast Heights, for a glow.

7001 Osuna Rd., NE, 505-884-7505, cabq.gov

TAKE A CLASS
AT HARWOOD ART CENTER

As one of the most vibrant destinations in the city, there's always something happening at the Harwood. It's a life-long learning center and a wing of Escuela del Sol Montessori, which, along with the school, artist studio buildings, and a gallery space, covers a full city block. The Harwood supports selected emerging artists through a professional development program, but even amateurs can take adult art classes here. Offerings include weekly open drawing sessions with a model, and scheduled oil painting, welding, and silversmithing courses. Perhaps these sessions will be your entrée into the art world and your work will hang in the handful of shows the Harwood staff curates each year.

1114 Seventh St., NW, 505-242-6367, harwoodartcenter.org

Neighborhood: Downtown

CRUISE
ROUTE 66

Follow the neon along eighteen miles of old Route 66 through Albuquerque. The historic Mother Road, now Central Avenue, bisects the city on its path from Chicago, Illinois to Los Angeles, California. Along the way, you'll pass some of the city's most popular neighborhoods and attractions, including Nob Hill, a trendy shopping area, the University of New Mexico, downtown and Old Town, the Rio Grande Botanical Garden and Albuquerque Aquarium, and past the volcanoes that hug the city's western edge. Take note of the intersection of Central and Fourth Street: Fourth Street was part of the original route (1926–1937) that ran north/south through Albuquerque along this existing road. In 1931, the route was realigned along an east/west trajectory. This is one of the few places that the two phases of the road intersect.

rt66nm.org

Neighborhood: Citywide
Kid Friendly

TIP
For the full vintage vibe, stop in 66 Diner (66diner.com) for a burger or a classic milkshake.

BUILD YOUR LOCAL TRIVIA KNOWLEDGE

WITH ALBUQUERQUE TROLLEY CO. AND ROUTES RENTALS & TOURS

Albuquerque has two top tour companies whose outings are as informative and entertaining for visitors as they are for locals. It's hard to beat the enthusiasm and local knowledge of the purveyors of these companies, but it's always worth a try!

On their open-air, stucco trolley, Jesse Herron and Mike Silva host eighty-five-minute "Best of ABQ City Tours." The tours are chock full of local history and tour several neighborhoods, giving insider views of the city's personality. The duo has also created themed excursions to the *Breaking Bad* filming locales, along an ale trail, and to see neon lights and urban art. Seasonal tours include the "Trolley of Terror," a Halloween tour, and the "Trolley of Lights," a ride through neighborhoods with exceptional holiday displays.

You'll often see Duke City natives and Routes Rentals & Tours owners, Heather and Josh Arnold, at the front of a pack of sunshine yellow and red cruiser bikes. Either they, or members of their friendly team of guides, lead cycling tours of the bosque daily. The company's themed outings include a Biking Bad tour, and those to local breweries and wineries. The company also guides excursions to the Albuquerque International Balloon Fiesta, through Old Town's luminarias on Christmas Eve, and for Valentine's Day. Whichever tour you take, you're sure to return with a new bit of local knowledge.

Neighborhood: Old Town
Kid Friendly

• •

Albuquerque Trolley Co.
800 Rio Grande Blvd., NW
(at Hotel Albuquerque)
505-240-8000
abqtrolley.com

Routes Rentals & Tours
404 San Felipe St., NW
505-933-5667
routesrentals.com

PURPLE UP
AT LAVENDER IN THE VILLAGE

Each July, Albuquerque does quite the impression of Provence, France, with row upon row of lavender in bloom. The village of Los Ranchos de Albuquerque makes the most of the season with a purple-passioned festival featuring gardening workshops, cooking demonstrations, and shopping for culinary and body lavender products at the Los Ranchos Growers' Market and field trips to the pick-it-yourself fields at Los Poblanos Inn and Organic Farm.

lavenderinthevillage.com, losranchosnm.gov/lavender-festival

Neighborhood: Los Ranchos de Albuquerque
Kid Friendly

TEST YOUR SHOPPING
CHOPS AT THE TURQUOISE MUSEUM

This small, privately owned museum explores all aspects of the color and stone that has so enraptured the Southwest. Members of the Lowry family, including the youngest, fifth generation, guide the forty-five-minute tours through the private museum. The tour begins by walking through a mock-mine where you can see how turquoise forms and is mined. Then you'll head into the collection room, which comprises only a small portion—four hundred pounds—of J. C. Zackary Jr.'s (a.k.a. the King of Turquoise) collection. The most dazzling specimen is the George Washington Stone, a chunk of turquoise that was cut into the shape of the founder's face on happy accident when preparing a piece for a hope chest. Subsequent rooms describe the process of staking a claim, how turquoise is rated for quality, and its cultural and spiritual history. If you're lucky, you'll tour when the on-site lapidary shop is in use, Robert A. Zachary and Joe Dan Lowry still create cabochons for the museum gift shop there. Guides are sure to establish the gem's rarity—only fifteen percent of the world's collection is hard enough to cut and polish—and how frequently it is stabilized, synthetically recreated, and, sometimes faked. Before you leave, you can browse the gift shop, which includes both natural (that's a key word to remember) and imitation turquoise, so you can practice your savvy shopping skills in a real-world environment.

2107 Central Ave., NW, 505-247-8650, turquoisemuseum.com

Neighborhood: Old Town
Kid Friendly

RIDE
THE HIGH-WIRE BIKE AT ¡EXPLORA!

Riding the second-story, high-wire bike at this science center is the closest that many Albuquerqueans will ever get to being in a circus act. Riders pedal the bike along an easy, out-and-back route high above the other hands-on exhibits, including those devoted to gravity, water, air, and arts and crafts. By day, the science center may be aimed at kids, but once a month, the center opens for an adults-only evening when the post-18 set can play in the bubbles without worrying about elbowing a toddler in an overly enthusiastic moment.

1701 Mountain Rd., NW, 505-224-8300, explora.us

Neighborhood: Old Town
Kid Friendly

BROWSE
516 ARTS

This independent, nonprofit contemporary arts organization displays some of the most intriguing and thought-provoking visual art in the city. The gallery setting is perfect for the installations and multimedia creations frequently displayed here. 516 also hosts a lively schedule of gallery talks, artist panels, workshops, and trunk shows. The organization has also made its mark on downtown's appearance with a series of murals on and near Central Avenue via 2010's *Street Arts: A Celebration of Hip Hop Culture and Free Expression.*

516 Central Ave., SW, 505-242-1445, 516arts.org

Neighborhood: Downtown

SWIM OVER TO THE
ABQ BIOPARK AQUARIUM

An aquarium in the desert? Yes, and a good one, too. The exhibits here cover habitats from the Río Grande to the Gulf Coast. Visitors love the ray pool and an arched eel tank you get to walk under. The favorite, however, is the 285,000-gallon shark tank. The Botanic Garden is on the same campus and can be toured during the same visit.

2601 Central Ave., NW, 505-768-2000, cabq.gov

Neighborhood: Old Town
Kid Friendly

BOTANIC GARDEN AGLOW
From approximately Thanksgiving through the new year, the grounds of the gardens glitter at River of Lights, featuring all manner of animatronic and statuesque creatures (from stegosaurus to Pegasus) in lights.

TIP

You and your kids can sleep with the sharks during Aquarium Overnights, held once a month on a Friday night. These events fill up nearly instantly, so take careful note of registration openings.

DRIVE
EL CAMINO REAL

Traveling the "royal road" is a trip through three hundred years of southwestern heritage. El Camino Real de Tierra Adentro traveled a route nearly as long as its formal name, sixteen hundred miles from Mexico City, Mexico, through what became the state of New Mexico. It was the earliest Euro-American trade route in the United States, and it brought as many Spanish colonists into today's New Mexico as it did goods. Today, you can drive sections of this historic route, including along NM 313 (a.k.a. Camino del Pueblo and El Camino Real) from the town of Bernalillo, which turns into Fourth Street in Albuquerque and extends to the south. Coronado Historic Site and Casa San Ysidro, described elsewhere in this book, are both along the route.

nps.gov/elca

Neighborhood: Bernalillo

LET WHIMSY TAKE OVER
AT TINKERTOWN MUSEUM

This is one of the most wonderfully wacky museums you'll ever encounter. Museum founder Ross Ward took more than forty years to carve and collect the mostly miniature wood-carved figures seen here—and to construct the unusual building constructed out of some fifty thousand glass bottles, as well as wagon wheels and horseshoes. The fifteen hundred figures are set in scenes such as a mining town and a circus, and kids (or you) can press buttons to see the vignettes come to life.

121 Sandia Crest Rd., 505-281-5233, tinkertown.com

Neighborhood: Sandia Park
Kid Friendly

TIP

This museum is open April through October. Have quarters on hand—or get them when you buy your ticket—so you can play Otto, the one-man band, and learn your future from Esmerelda the animatronic fortuneteller, á la Tom Hanks in *Big*.

MAKE YOUR WAY
TO MADRID

Driving the Turquoise Trail National Scenic Byway, on the east side of the Sandia Mountains, is the perfect day trip from the Duke City. The charming town of Madrid is a pleasant waypoint along the route. On Sundays, local motorcyclists flock in droves to the Mine Shaft Tavern for a burger and live music. The tavern is a throwback to the town's roots, but today there are more artists here than miners. You can spend an afternoon zigzagging across NM 14 to the galleries and eclectic shops that line the scenic route, including mainstays such as The Johnsons of Madrid, Indigo Gallery, and Studio 14, the latter of which represents more than twenty local artists. For a caffeinated pick-me-up—or a night's stay in the bed and breakfast—stop in Java Junction. Some of the best bites in town are the southern-fried selections at The Hollar.

TIP
The Madrid and Cerrillos Studio Tour is held each October and offers the chance to meet artists in their homes and workspaces.

MADRID HOT SPOTS

The Hollar
2849 NM 14, 505-471-4821
thehollar.com

Java Junction
2855 NM 14, 505-438-2772
java-junction.com

The Johnsons of Madrid
2843 NM 14, 505-471-1054

Indigo Gallery
2854 NM 14, Ste. D, 505-438-6202
indigoartgallery.com

Mine Shaft Tavern
2846 NM 14, 505-473-0743
themineshafttavern.com

Studio 14
2860 NM 14, 505-474-6360
studio14madrid.com

FEEL AT HOME
AT CASA SAN YSIDRO

Stepping across the threshold at Casa San Ysidro: The Gutiérrez/ Minge House feels like coming home. The Gutiérrez family first owned the historic adobe, circa 1875, but since that time, it has been added on to and romantically recreated—just as many other homes in the city have been. Alan and Shirley Minge bought the home in the 1950s and fashioned a well-researched version of a nineteenth-century rancho, a small chapel, a plazuela, and an enclosed corral using pieces Dr. Minge collected from all over the state, including wooden doors from the Duranes family chapel in Talpa and corbels from a church in Tomé. Dr. and Mrs. Minge also compiled an extensive collection of New Mexican art and furnishings—now considered one of the world's most comprehensive. The artifacts are all the more intriguing because they're displayed in scenic surroundings. The collection includes stunning tinwork, bultos, and retablos, rare copper cosas (kitchen tubs), including one dated 1689, a hand-carved Velarde chest, and a loom from 1775, among other treasures.

973 Old Church Road, 505-898-3915, cabq.gov/casasanysidro

Neighborhood: Corrales
Kid Friendly

TIP

Casa is closed in December and January. When open, it's only accessible via scheduled tours, plan your visit accordingly. Casa's biggest events each year are Heritage Day, held in May around the time of the Feast Day of San Ysidro, and Harvest Weekend, a village-wide celebration the last weekend of September.

TOUR
THE TAMARIND INSTITUTE

Although it may be below the radar of many Albuquerqueans, the Tamarind Institute has a world-class reputation in the art of lithography. A division of the College of Fine Arts at the University of New Mexico, the institute runs a second-story gallery space that mounts a handful of shows each year. But this is also a working print shop that runs a professional program, sponsoring eight students and two apprentices a year who earn their master printer certificates, and facilitates the work of invited artists, who, though celebrated in their respective media, may be creating a lithograph for the first time. Artists who have worked at the institute during its more than fifty-year history (it was founded in 1960 in Los Angeles and moved to Albuquerque in 1970) include former associate director Clinton Adams and former technical director Garo Antreasian, Hung Liu, and Jim Dine. The institute offers ninety-minute tours on the first Friday of most months that guide you through the professional and student sides of the print shop, and demonstrate the lithography process in which an artist creates an image on a—in this case— stone, inks the plate, and pulls an impression.

2500 Central Ave., SE, 505-277-3901, tamarind.unm.edu

Neighborhood: University

TIP

If you want to explore the institute's full archives, the University of New Mexico Art Museum, described elsewhere in this guide, keeps an archive of every print created since the institute's founding. The archives can be viewed by appointment.

PLUG INTO THE
OLD TOWN TREE LIGHTING

Albuquerque's Plaza Don Luis may not be Rockefeller Center, but it comes pretty close when the fifty-five-foot-tall tree is alight there each December. The tree is actually made up of one hundred thirty smaller trees assembled to look like a towering pine. The tree lighting coincides with the Old Town Merchants Association Shop and Stroll, when stores stay open late for holiday shopping.

Plaza Don Luis, cabq.gov, albuquerqueoldtown.com

Neighborhood: Old Town
Kid Friendly

WATCH THE CORRALES
FOURTH OF JULY PARADE

This pastoral village, just north of Albuquerque, presents a charming Independence Day parade. Anyone is welcome to join—whether two or four legged. Town residents parade with their dogs, alpacas, donkeys, rabbits, and even chickens—all decked out in red, white, and blue for the occasion, of course. You'll also see vintage trucks and bagpipe—and the slightly less baritone kazoo—bands. Bring your own chair and pick a spot along Corrales Road, the main thoroughfare here, after the parade, join the festivities at La Entrada Park.

corralesjuly4.com

Neighborhood: Corrales
Kid Friendly

BLUFF UP
AT ACOMA PUEBLO'S SKY CITY

Visiting the spectacular Sky City, an adobe Puebloan village perched on a sandstone bluff above the valley floor, makes for an extraordinary day trip. Inhabited since 1150 A.D., the pueblo is one of the longest continuously occupied communities in the United States. Visitors can't wander freely around Acoma Pueblo, so check out the Cultural Center and Haa'ku Museum to purchase your tour ticket to Sky City. Although there are some five thousand members of Acoma Pueblo, about forty-five people reside year-round on the seventy-acre mesa top. A tour bus will then transport you to the mesa's summit and a guide will lead you among the traditional residences and past kivas (ceremonial chambers). A tour highlight is stepping inside San Estevan del Rey Mission, a National Historic Landmark. One of the largest churches of its kind, it still features the original altar and works of art that date to its 1629–1640 construction. Be sure to descend back to the cultural center via the stone staircase, which Puebloan ancestors once used as their sole access to and from their homes.

Fifty miles west of Albuquerque off I-40, (800) 747-0181
acomaskycity.org

TIP

The annual San Esteban
del Rey feast day is September 2,
when the pueblo honors its
patron saint with masses,
afternoon corn dances,
and an arts-and-crafts fair.

GET PC
AT THE NEW MEXICO MUSEUM OF NATURAL HISTORY & SCIENCE

Picture the birthplace of the personal computer and you may instantly picture Seattle. In fact, Albuquerque played a crucial role in the creation of our modern way of life. In "Start Up: Albuquerque and the Personal Computer Revolution," you'll learn how Bill Gates and Paul Allen first incorporated Micro-Soft (they later changed the spelling) in the Duke City and discover the duo's early years (1975–1978) working on the eighth floor of Two Park Central Tower. The exhibit includes programming tapes, letters, notes, and other memorabilia—it doesn't include, however, Bill Gates' mug shot from when he was arrested for a traffic violation.

The Museum of Natural History & Science's permanent exhibits also walk you through twelve billion years of natural history, from the formation of the universe through the dawn of the dinosaurs (and the age of the super giants), the age when New Mexico was a seascape, and through the Ice Age. The museum also includes a planetarium and the DynaTheater, where you can see IMAX style shows.

1801 Mountain Rd., NW, 505-841-2800, nmnaturalhistory.org

Neighborhood: Old Town
Kid Friendly

TIP
The museum is free to New Mexico residents on the first Sunday of the month.

TAKE A GHOST TOUR
OF OLD TOWN

Whether you're ready to see a specter or just skeptical, this tour is an enjoyable way to learn about the city's past. Guided by Tours of Old Town, this walk through Albuquerque's founding neighborhood will take you past the ill-chosen former location of the town graveyard, the past home of the undertaker, High Noon Restaurant and Saloon, and down "Scarlett's Alley" to hear chill-inducing ghost stories. The tales, which include mention of trappers, Confederate soldiers, prostitutes, and blue-collar workers, reflect the many phases of the neighborhood's past—beginning when Albuquerque was just four blocks across.

Plaza Don Luis, 303 Romero St., NW, 505-246-8687

toursofoldtown.com

Neighborhood: Old Town

TIP
Reservations for the nightly tours are required. Tours of Old Town also offers once-a-month moonlight tours at a later time. Spook Troop tours for junior ghost hunters aged six to twelve years offer softer versions of the ghost stories.

SHOPPING AND FASHION

GET HEARTY AND HALE

AT LOCAL GROWERS' MARKETS

The Downtown Growers' Market and the Rail Yards Market are the city's top shops for fresh-from-the-field produce. The downtown market, held on Saturdays, has a larger number of participating farmers, with regulars such as Skarsgard Farms (operators of the state's largest CSA) and Wagner Farms. At the Rail Yards Market, held on Sundays in the revitalized blacksmith shop of the once-derelict rail yards, producers such as Vecinos del Bosque keep Albuquerqueans stocked up on arugula, carrots, and tomatoes, to name a few. The markets also sell prepared foods, including sweets from the New Mexico Pie Company and treats for Fido from Tailwaggin' Temptations. Craftspeople set up shop here too, selling homemade soaps and lotions, jewelry, and pottery. The markets aren't just places to shop, they're also community gathering spots for neighbors and friends. At the downtown market, families sprawl on blankets in the grass of Robinson Park and kids kick up their heels to live bluegrass music. At the Rail Yards Market, bystanders can watch—or join in with—bellydancers or folklorico dancers at the community stage, and watch a children's play or listen to poetry on the main stage.

Downtown Growers' Market
Eighth St. and Central Ave., 505-243-2230, downtowngrowers.com

Rail Yards Market
777 First St., SW, railyardsmarket.org

Neighborhoods: Downtown and Barelas
Kid Friendly

CHARGE DOWN
TO OLD TOWN

A trip to this tree-lined plaza is first on many visitors' lists—and there are plenty of tourist-focused trinket shops to prove it. (Hey, sometimes you just need a zia t-shirt!) But among the one hundred fifty shops there are plenty of galleries and boutiques, too. You may also shop from the Puebloan and Navajo craftspeople who lay out blankets with their wares on the east side of the plaza. You'll easily spend a few hours wandering down cobblestone pathways and through small courtyards off the plaza, such as that at Poco a Poco Patio.

albuquerqueoldtown.com

Neighborhood: Old Town
Kid Friendly

DON'T MISS
Although it may not be on your shopping agenda, stop in San Felipe de Neri Church. When Albuquerque was founded in 1706, the first building erected was a church. Although not the original building, this house of worship has been in almost continuous use for nearly three hundred years. The intimate Chapel of Our Lady of Guadalupe (404 San Felipe St., NW at Patio Escondito) is also worth visiting.

OLD TOWN SHOPPING LIST

Albuquerque Photographers' Gallery: This artist co-op includes some of the city's best artists—and you'll find stunning pictures of the state's landscapes and people here.

Plaza Don Luis: 303 Romero St., NW, Ste. #208
505-244-9195, abqphotographersgallery.com

Church Street Café: this restaurant in a historic adobe serves authentic—and delicious—New Mexican fare.

2111 Church St., NW, 505-247-8522, churchstreetcafe.com

Matí: for contemporary jewelry, the sparkling opals and diamonds at Matí by international design house Kabana may catch your eye.

201 Romero St., NW, 505-244-1595, matijewelers.com

Tanner Chaney Galleries: In business since 1875, this gallery has fine Native American jewelry, pottery, and rugs. They also offer a healthy collection of estate and pawn jewelry, which offer fine opportunities for bargains.

323 Romero St., NW, 505-247-2242, tannerchaney.com

Weems Galleries and Framing
This is one of the city's top galleries, its Old Town location features Southwestern-inspired paintings, ceramic and jewelry.

Plaza Don Luis: 303 Romero St., NW, 505-764-0302,
weemsgallery.com

PICK UP A BAUBLE
AT GERTRUDE ZACHARY JEWELRY

Although groundbreaking businesswoman Gertrude Zachary (1937–2013) passed away, she left a brightly colored stamp on southwest jewelry. She and her daughter, Erica Hatchell, who has also taken up the design mantel, are known for contemporary, southwest creations in a field that men long dominated. Zachary particularly enjoyed bold, statement pieces—from chunky turquoise necklaces to eye-catching coral cuffs. Her stores (one in Nob Hill, one in Old Town) offer so many glittering choices, it may be difficult to pick just one.

1501 Lomas Blvd., NW, 505-247-4442
3300 Central Ave., SE, 505-766-4700, gertrudezachary.com

Neighborhoods: Old Town and Nob Hill

MAKE A PILGRIMAGE
TO SKIP MAISEL'S INDIAN JEWELRY

This go-to spot for Native American jewelry and pottery has reached landmark status in the city. Maurice Maisel started this store in 1923 and moved into its current location in 1939, in a building designed by noted architect John Gaw Meem. You may be here to shop, but before you get to the bargains inside, linger in the T-shaped entrance. Here, contractor John McDowell set a thunderbird of crushed turquoise and coral in the terrazzo floor. Above the window displays, murals created by students of Dorothy Dunn, of the Santa Fe Indian School, depict Navajo, deer, butterfly, and corn dancers; an antelope hunt; and other cultural vignettes. Inside, most of this wholesalers' prices are half-off retail, so you'll find great deals on Navajo, Jemez, and Acoma pottery, and traditional southwestern jewelry in every hue from multi-strand, turquoise heishis to coral squash blossom necklaces.

510 Central Ave., SW, 505-242-6526, skipmaisels.com

Neighborhood: Downtown

HOBNOB
IN NOB HILL

Named after Nob Hill in San Francisco, this is one of the city's most vibrant restaurant and shopping districts.

route66central.com

Neighborhood: Nob Hill

NOB HILL SHOPPING LIST

Beeps
Mary Reed opened Beeps in 1985 and immediately started stocking an inventory of oddities from ironic T-shirts to mustache stickers. This is the best place in town for irreverent birthday cards and gifts that will have you wondering how you or someone you know ever lived with out that rubber-chicken purse.

3500 Central Ave., SE
505-262-1900
on Facebook

Izzy Martin Menswear
This hip men's clothing boutique outfits some of the best-dressed gents in town.

3019 Central Ave., NE
505-232-9223
izzymartin.com

Mariposa Gallery
This contemporary crafts gallery curates a collection that lives up to its tag line: curiouser and curiouser. Pulling from its stable of represented artists and guests, the gallery also presents monthly exhibits.

3500 Central Ave., SE
505-268-6828
mariposa-gallery.com

Masks y Mas
The Mexican holiday Día de Los Muertos (Day of the Dead) may only come once a year, but you can celebrate it year-round in this art gallery specializing in papier-mâché skulls, *catrinas* (skeleton sculptures), and indigenous masks from around the world.

3106 Central Ave., SE
505-256-4183
masksymas.net

SchuShop
This women's accessories shop stocks affordable shoes, handbags, and scarves in a friendly, boutique setting.

109-B Carlisle Blvd., SE
505-503-8594
schushopabq.com

Toad Road
A men's and women's clothing boutique, Toad Road offers brand names and items from local designers with a dash of vintage finds for good measure.

3503 Central Ave., NE
505-255-4212

HISTORICAL HIGHLIGHTS

Nob Hill was platted for development in 1916, just four years after New Mexico became a state. It is bordered by Lomas Boulevard to the north, Washington Street to the east, Zuni Road and Garfield Avenue to the south, and Girard Boulevard to the west. Here are a few buildings to note while browsing:

Nob Hill Shopping Center
Designed by noted architect Louis Hesselden, this shopping center boasts the iconic "Nob Hill" sign, and was designed with a mixture of Territorial Revival and Moderne elements. Today, it's home to Scalo, a northern Italian grill; La Montanita Co-Op; SchuShop, and Beeps; among others.

3500 Central Ave., SE

Immanuel Presbyterian Church
Renowned architecture John Gaw Meem designed this working church in 1949. It exudes what came to be known as the Territorial Revival style.

114 Carlisle Blvd., SE

Kelly's Brew Pub
On summer evenings Kelly's patio is packed with revelers sipping craft beer and noshing on nachos. At one time, however, there were more Fords than frolickers on this patio. In 1939, Ralph Jones commissioned a Ford dealership and service station to be the home of the Jones Motor Company. The building, a fine example of the Streamline Moderne architectural style, is now listed on the National Register of Historic Places.

3222 Central Ave., SE

Monte Vista Fire Station Restaurant
There's truth in advertising in this restaurant's name: the building was formerly a fire station. Architect Ernst Blumenthal incorporated Spanish-Pueblo Revival elements in this structure's design; it was built in 1936 under the WPA.

3201 Central Ave., NE

ATTEND AN AUTHOR
READING AT BOOKWORKS

This locally owned, indie bookstore has a calendar that would be the envy of any socialite: it hosts upwards of four hundred events annually, from author talks and readings, to journaling and writing workshops. Since 1984, the bookstore has stocked reads by national, best-selling authors. It also keeps a hearty helping of titles by New Mexico and southwest writers of every genre.

4022 Rio Grande Blvd., NW, 505-344-8139, bkwrks.com

Neighborhood: North Valley
Kid Friendly *(depending on the author)*

Another Indie Bookstore Favorite:
Page One Books, 5850 Eubank Blvd., NE, Ste. B41
505-294-2026, page1book.com

Neighborhood: North East Heights

SUGGESTED
ITINERARIES
(listed by page number)

• •

DATE NIGHT

FAMILIES

• •

• •

GIRLS' DAY OR NIGHT OUT

GREAT OUTDOORS

• •

• •

ACTIVITIES BY SEASON
(listed by page number)

ANYTIME

• •

• •

FALL

SPRING

SUMMER

• •

WINTER

ACTIVITIES
BY NEIGHBORHOOD
(listed by page number)

BARELAS

CITYWIDE

DOWNTOWN

• •

EDO

FOOTHILLS

INTERNATIONAL DISTRICT

LOS RANCHOS DE ALBUQUERQUE

MESA DEL SOL

NOB HILL

NORTH VALLEY

NORTHEAST HEIGHTS

OLD TOWN

• •

ROAD TRIPS

SOUTH VALLEY

• •

UNIVERSITY

UPTOWN

WELLS PARK

WESTSIDE

• •

INDEX

• •

• •

● ●